Lead Yourself First

Lead Yourself First

INSPIRING LEADERSHIP THROUGH SOLITUDE

with a foreword by Jim Collins

RAYMOND M. KETHLEDGE AND MICHAEL S. ERWIN

B L O O M S B U R Y

NEW YORK · LONDON · OXFORD · NEW DELHI · SYDNEY

Bloomsbury USA
An imprint of Bloomsbury Publishing Plc

1385 Broadway   50 Bedford Square
New York   London
NY 10018   WC1B 3DP
USA   UK

www.bloomsbury.com

BLOOMSBURY and the Diana logo are trademarks of Bloomsbury
Publishing Plc

First published 2017

ISBN: HB: 978-1-63286-631-8
       ePub: 978-1-63286-633-2

LIBRARY OF CONGRESS CATALOGING-IN-PUBLICATION DATA

Names: Kethledge, Raymond Michael, author. | Erwin, Michael S., author.
Title: Lead yourself first : inspiring leadership with solitude / with a foreword
by Jim Collins ; Raymond M. Kethledge and Michael S. Erwin.
Description: New York : Bloomsbury USA, 2017.
Identifiers: LCCN 2016044432 | ISBN 9781632866318 (hardcover : alk. paper)
Subjects: LCSH: Leadership. | Leadership—Case studies.
Classification: LCC HD57.7 .K47766 2017 | DDC 658.4/092—dc23 LC record
available at https://lccn.loc.gov/2016044432

2 4 6 8 10 9 7 5 3 1

Typeset by RefineCatch Limited, Bungay, Suffolk
Printed and bound in the U.S.A. by Berryville Graphics Inc., Berryville, Virginia

To reflective leaders, present and future

"We live, in fact, in an age starved for solitude."

—C. S. LEWIS

Contents

A Note About Structure

This book is based on the experiences of leaders—some contemporary, some historical—who have used solitude to function more effectively as leaders. Our research has been qualitative: rather than gather large masses of data (say, from survey results) and then look for patterns within that data, we have gathered the stories of individual leaders and looked for patterns within those. Qualitative research takes longer than quantitative research; in our case, about five years. But our research has revealed patterns nonetheless. Some of those patterns concern the different purposes for which leaders use solitude: broadly stated, to find clarity, creativity, emotional balance, and moral courage. Other patterns concern the different ways in which leaders find solitude, and the obstacles they face in finding it.

Our research began, in a sense, with our own experiences. Although Mike is a strong extrovert and Ray a strong introvert, both of us have sought out solitude throughout our adult lives. As a first lieutenant in Iraq during 2004, Mike chose to walk rather than ride each day to the chow hall, a mile each way, twice a day, in temperatures approaching 100 degrees. In those days Mike had a dozen soldiers reporting to him, on a base repeatedly attacked by mortar and rocket fire. Sometimes, on those walks, Mike gathered his thoughts about some problem then facing him. Other times, he steadied himself emotionally. Years later, during the solitude of long runs, Mike developed the idea for a new nonprofit to support

veterans returning home from deployments overseas. Now known as
Team Red, White & Blue, the nonprofit benefits more than a
hundred thousand veterans. Ray found solitude, as a law student,
during solo camping trips in the forests of northern Michigan, fish-
ing in the streams there. As a law clerk to Justice Anthony Kennedy,
Ray walked alone around the Capitol and the Supreme Court building when thinking through a case. Now, as a federal judge, Ray heads
up to his barn office looking out on northern Lake Huron, without
any Internet connection, when writing opinions in difficult cases.

With the exception of one story about Mike, however, this book
is based on the stories of other leaders. We define leadership
broadly, to include running a large corporation with thousands of
employees, or leading a handful of employees on a single team, or
leading a single family member through crisis or growth. Anyone
who leads anyone—including oneself—can benefit from solitude.
About half the book is based on interview material from contemporary leaders—some of them famous, but more of them people
like the readers of this book. Other chapters illustrate the experiences of prominent leaders throughout history—Eisenhower in
the days before D-day, Aung San Suu Kyi during her years of house
arrest in Burma, Martin Luther King Jr. during the Montgomery
bus boycott, to name a few. Each of those chapters tells a discrete
story about how the leader used solitude to be more effective. In
some of these stories, the leader used solitude as a regular practice,
as Eisenhower did when he wrote memoranda to himself during
World War II. Other stories show how a leader used solitude in a
particular instance, as Martin Luther King did at his kitchen table
one night in January 1956. But all of these stories are stories, rather
than snapshots. And thus each of them involves a discussion not
only of solitude itself, but also of the broader circumstances—the
time, the setting, the difficulties—in which the leader found
himself or herself. Taken as a whole, however, each of those chapters provides an illustration of the timeless importance of solitude
to effective leadership.

The book is divided into four parts, each of them focusing upon
a particular quality—clarity, creativity, emotional balance, and

moral courage—that solitude enhances. Our discussion of interview material tracks those boundaries, and for the most part the historical chapters do as well. But sometimes a historical story that primarily illustrates one quality also touches upon another. Eisenhower's story is about clarity, for example, but to a lesser extent shows how he used solitude to maintain his emotional balance. We keep those stories intact rather than separate the different parts of the story into different parts of the book.

What our contemporary and historical research has shown above all, however, is that personal leadership—leading oneself—is the foundation of leading others. And personal leadership comes through solitude.

Foreword by Jim Collins

Leading from good to great requires discipline—disciplined people who engage in disciplined thought and who take disciplined action. To engage in disciplined action first requires disciplined thought, and disciplined thought requires people who have the discipline to create quiet time for reflection. The net result is not doing more, but doing less. Stop-doing lists reflect greater discipline than ever-expanding to-do lists of frenetic activity. This book is all about creating those pockets and putting them to good use.

When Darwin Smith served as chief executive of Kimberly-Clark, he made many of his biggest strategic decisions in "tractor time." He would visit his farm in Wisconsin, rumbling around on a tractor backhoe, picking up gigantic rocks from a pile, and moving them across the property to another pile. At one crucial point, he faced a conundrum: what to do about the struggling paper-mills business that had anchored the company for a hundred years. Smith mulled around for a long time, moving rocks from pile to pile, then back again. And he gained clarity: "If you have a cancer in your arm, you have to have the guts to cut off your own arm," reflected Smith, who had once battled throat cancer. He made a clear decision: Sell the mills—jettison a hundred years of legacy—and put all the resources into the company's emerging consumer business, going all-in with a big bet on consumer-facing brands like Kleenex. A board member called it one of the gutsiest decisions he'd ever seen a CEO make, a turning point that ignited a good-to-great transformation and earned Smith a spot as one of the greatest business leaders of the twentieth century.

Winston Churchill loved to lay bricks at Chartwell, his home retreat, especially when cast into his "wilderness years" of the 1930s. Bill Gates, during the rise of Microsoft, set aside entire weeks to just go away and read and reflect, what he called "think week." Warren Buffett gravitated toward the quietude of his hometown of Omaha, Nebraska, and crafted a simple daily life full of reading and gestation; one of Buffett's fondest phrases: "Inactivity can be very intelligent behavior." George Washington would lose himself for hours riding his favorite horse around Mount Vernon. Ron Chernow's fabulous biography of Washington tells of how he thrived on a daily routine of unvarying regularity, making particular use of time alone for work and reflection early in the morning before others awoke. Chernow also questions the famous image of Washington on his knees in prayerful meditation at Valley Forge, seeking guidance and strength, oblivious to people around him— not because he doubted the act but because Washington would have almost certainly done so alone, in private.

Of course, you need not be in such rarified company to make use of quiet solitude. While working on this foreword, I am completing a study of exceptional people who lead K–12 schools to high results in the most difficult and adverse circumstances, from dangerous urban neighborhoods to poor rural townships. These K–12 school leaders continually renew themselves for redeployment day by day and year by year; many do so by creating alone-time to reflect and recharge. One elementary principal in a school whose students come from an adjacent, crime-ridden neighborhood crafted a personal bubble every morning, just sitting in her car, before heading into the building. She deliberately arrived a few minutes early whenever possible, to give herself these moments.

The key, as the authors illustrate with their marvelous collection of case studies, is to develop two practices. First, systematically build pockets of solitude into your life. We all have no more than twenty-four hours in a day, and they will be chewed up unless you deliberately structure time for solitude, inserting some "white space" in your calendar. White space does not mean vacation; it simply means nothing scheduled. Think of it as like putting down rocks in the river; if you wait for the river to stop flowing before you walk out and put a rock down, you'll never get one out there. Instead, better to drop a rock in the flow and make the river go around it. This is the idea of white space, time scheduled with yourself, honored as you would any other vital appointment. The second discipline is to recognize unexpected opportunities for solitude and seize them. It might come in the form of an unexpected life change that pulls you out of the fray, or it might come in a more pedestrian form. What do you do when stuck in traffic or with an unexpected flight delay? What do you do when you've been gifted an unexpected twenty minutes before a meeting? What do you do when you wake up earlier than others in the morning or find yourself awake late at night? Do you capture the opportunity for quiet solitude, or do you run from it?

I admire people who apply their writings to their own lives in leadership. When Michael Erwin served as an intelligence officer, deployed into combat zones after 9/11, he held responsibility for processing intelligence information that had bearing on lives and missions. "The amount of information could be just overwhelming—data, signals, intelligence reports, information from people—and I had to build in a place to be by myself to reflect," he once told me. "So, I would go out and do a long run in 100-plus-degree heat, doing circles in a wire-enclosed three-mile loop. It was the one place I could go to find that meditative state to get clear." In one crucial case, Erwin gained the clarity and summoned the strength to argue for an interpretation different from higher-ranking officers'. He won the argument and was proven right by events, thereby increasing the odds of a successful mission.

Leadership is the art of getting people to want to do what must be done, in the keen insight of General Eisenhower. And the X factor that distinguishes truly great leaders is not personality but a paradoxical combination of humility and will in service to a cause bigger than the personal ambitions of that leader. This is the distinctive trait of what in our good-to-great research we came to call

"Level 5 Leadership." Solitude can play a catalytic role in gaining clarity about what must be done and summoning the fierce resolve to carry through, a centering place where the seeds of Level 5 can gestate and begin to flower. The courageous action—the leadership action—requires not bravado but objective equanimity and calm clarity.

We live in a cacophonous age, swarming insects of noise and interruption buzzing about—e-mails, text messages, cable news, advertisements, cell phones, meetings, wireless Web connections, social media posts, and all the new intrusions invented by the time you are reading this. If leadership begins not with what you do but with who you are, then when and how do you escape the noise to find your purpose and summon the strength to pursue it? This book illustrates how leaders can—indeed must—be disciplined people who create the quiet space for disciplined thought and summon the strength for disciplined action. It is a message needed now more than ever, else we run the risk of waking up at the end of the year having accomplished little of significance, each year slipping by in a flurry of activity pointing nowhere. So take some quiet time, engage with this book, and commit to the hard work of time alone.

Jim Collins
Boulder, Colorado
July 17, 2016

Introduction

To lead others, you must first lead yourself. That, ultimately, is the theme of this book.

Leadership, as Dwight Eisenhower defined it, is "the art of getting someone else to do something that you want done because he wants to do it." That does not mean that leadership amounts to using people; like anyone else, a leader must recognize that each person is an end in himself. It means, instead, to make others embrace your goals as their own. But to do that you must first determine your goals. And you must do that with enough clarity and conviction to hold fast to your goals—even when, inevitably, there are great pressures to yield from them. To develop that clarity and conviction of purpose, and the moral courage to sustain it through adversity, requires something that one might not associate with leadership. That something is solitude.

Solitude in this sense is not merely physical separation from others or togetherness with nature, although for some people it might involve those things. Solitude, as the term is used here, can be found as readily while sitting alone in a restaurant as it can on Mount Rainier. It is not an objective concept but a subjective one. It is, simply, a subjective *state of mind*, in which the mind, *isolated from input from other minds*, works through a problem on its own. That isolation can be sustained, as it was for Thoreau or is for a long-distance runner. Or it can be intermittent, as it might be for a person who reads a book—which of course is a collection of someone else's thoughts—and then pauses occasionally to think through a passage's meaning. But what comes in between those moments of isolation must focus the mind, rather than distract it.

For solitude in this sense—the leadership sense—is hard work. Not the phony work of a clattering keyboard in response to an e-mailed lunch invitation, or a furrowed brow while surfing the Net. Instead, leadership solitude is productive solitude, which means to use solitude purposely, with a particular end in mind. Productive solitude involves working your mind—not passively, but actively, as you would a large muscle—as you break down and sort and synthesize what is already there. When that process of work and isolation is successful—and when done honestly, it usually is—the result is an insight, or even a broader vision, that brings mind and soul together in clear-eyed, inspired conviction. And that kind of conviction is the foundation of leadership.

For genuine leadership means taking the harder path. There are plenty of easier ones: the worn path of convention, smooth and obstacle-free; the fenced path of bureaucracy, where all the hard thinking is done for you, so long as you go wherever it leads; and the parade route of adulation, for those who elevate their followers' approval above all. To depart from any of these paths takes a considered act of will. Not because they are plainly right— more often the opposite is true—but because of the consequences that are sure to follow. The leader who defies convention must bear the disapproval of establishment types, who will try to coerce him morally, and failing that might box his ears. The leader who defies bureaucracy is usually in for harder treatment, as its machinery, given the chance, will run over him with the indifference of a tank. And the leader who makes unpopular decisions must be willing to be unpopular herself, at least for a while.

Virtually no one seeks out these consequences for their own sake. The leaders who bear them do so in furtherance of a larger vision—one that comes from within. That is where solitude plays its role. Solitude yields the clarity to know when the easy path is the wrong one. And solitude, through its fusion of mind and soul, produces within the leader the stronger alloy of conviction, which in turn braces her with the moral courage *not* to conform, and to bear the consequences that result.

All of these consequences, moreover, lie in the rear. Out front, more often than not, lies adversity in the usual sense, in the form of painful costs, setbacks, mistakes in execution, and initial if not repeated failures. An empty vessel of a leader will break apart in those storms. The leader fortified with solitude can withstand them.

All of which suggests that the foundations of leadership are in jeopardy today. For if an essential element of solitude is mental isolation, its antithesis is accessibility; and the minds of our leaders today are accessible as never before. The point hardly needs elaboration: e-mails, texts, tweets, and the rest, not to mention the Internet itself, all swarm about the leader (and almost everyone else) with input from other minds. There are benefits to that phenomenon— some of the bites, so to speak, are salutary—but a central point of this book is that, for the leader especially, there ought to be a lot more screened-off areas than there are now.

The problem goes beyond the loss of isolation. The bulk of these inputs are, by their nature, superficial: messages about where to meet, what to eat, what to buy, or stray fragments of thought that, in different times, might at least have been organized into a coherent whole. These inputs distract the mind to no end, tying it down to the mere surface of thought, like a thousand Lilliputians. They do the same to the soul, keeping us from drilling down to where reserves of inspiration lie. Serious thinking, inspired thinking, can seldom arise from texts sent while eating lunch or driving a car. Responding to these inputs generates as much thought, and as much inspiration, as swatting so many flies. They deaden both the mind and soul.

Another problem concerns not the means by which we communicate today, but the manner. It is commonplace now to yell rather than speak, to talk over each other rather than listen, to answer criticism without pausing to consider whether it has merit. Our culture has become more strident than sublime, with a coarseness that has worn away the delicate alloy of beauty and decency that used to be called grace. But there is still grace in solitude, and oftentimes sublimity too. The examples of history—Lincoln, Churchill, Martin

Luther King—show that a sublime leader is a more effective one, with an ability to inspire his followers rather than incite them, to the betterment of everyone concerned.

But these problems have a solution. In years past, leaders used solitude without even being aware of the fact. Today it takes a conscious effort. One part of the solution is simply discipline—the discipline to unplug, to make oneself inaccessible, cleanly and without peeking—which takes moral courage, too, since these days that defies convention. The other part, indeed the part that must come first, is awareness—awareness of what we lose with accessibility, of what is lost inside—to the detriment, ultimately, of leadership. Among other things.

This book aims to retake this ground.

PART I

CHAPTER 1

Clarity

Of all the decisions Dwight Eisenhower ever made as a leader, none was more important than his decision to launch the D-day invasion on June 6, 1944, rather than two weeks later. That decision brought great risk: at the time Eisenhower made it, there was a strong possibility that the weather would prevent any reinforcements from landing on June 7, in which case the troops who landed the day before might be pushed out to sea. But a decision to delay the invasion would have brought great risks of a different sort, not least that the Germans would find out where the Allies planned to land. Eisenhower had to weigh all those risks, and choose between them. He did so only after obtaining—through deliberate effort—the greatest possible clarity as to which choice offered the best chance of success.

Clarity is often a difficult thing for a leader to obtain. Concerns of the present tend to loom larger than potentially greater concerns that lie farther away. Some decisions by their nature present great complexity, whose many variables must align a certain way for the leader to succeed. Compounding the difficulty, now more than ever, is what ergonomists call information overload, where a leader is overrun with inputs—via e-mails, meetings, and phone calls—that only distract and clutter his thinking. Alternatively, the leader's information might be only fragmentary, which might cause her to fill in the gaps with assumptions—sometimes without recognizing them as such. And the merits of a leader's most important decisions, by their nature, typically are not clear-cut. Instead those decisions involve "a process of assigning weights to competing interests, and then determining, based upon some criterion, which one predominates. The result is one of judgment, of shades of gray; like saying that Beethoven is a better composer than Brahms."

Solitude offers ways for leaders to obtain greater clarity. A leader who thinks through a complex problem by hard analytical work—as Eisenhower did before D-day—can identify the conditions necessary to solve it. A leader who silences the din not only around her mind, but inside it, can then hear the delicate voice of intuition, which may have already made connections that her conscious mind has not. And a leader who is aware of his weaknesses can guard against them.

Other benefits are more spiritual, but no less important because of it. The best work is inspired work. A reflective leader will ask not only what decision she should make, but whether and how her actions advance some larger purpose. A party of mountain climbers does not seek merely to climb the mountain. A teacher can teach his students more than just the subject of his class. A parent of a child with special needs might find profound meaning in the struggles of her child and herself alike. The most inspiring leaders are ones who find a clarity of meaning that transcends the tasks at hand. And that meaning emerges through reflection.

THE FOUNDATION OF both analytical and intuitive clarity is an uncluttered mind. Bill George illustrates one way to obtain it. George was a highly successful CEO of Medtronic Inc., among other executive positions. He now teaches at Harvard Business School and is the author of the bestselling *True North*, in which he advocates that leaders reflect on their core values as a means of setting the vector of their leadership.

"A critical element of effective leadership is not to let the immediate take precedence over the important," George says. "Today's world puts too much emphasis on the immediate. That's a perpetual danger for leaders." George emphasizes that reflection is not only for introverts. "I'm a very active, extroverted person who likes to get a lot done," he says. "In my thirties I was going strong, doing well in my career, with one child and another on the way." But in those days his energy was spent before he came home each day. "I'd work until seven or eight each night, eat dinner, read a magazine, and then zone out."

Around that time, however, George began a daily meditation practice, specifically transcendental meditation. He says, "I don't know how TM works, but it does. TM allows you to slow down, to reflect. As a relaxation process, and a process for introspection, it couldn't be better."

The process of transcendental meditation is simple. The practitioner (i.e., the person meditating) ideally meditates for two twenty-minute sessions per day, one before the workday and one near the end of it, though even one session is vastly better than none. During each session, the practitioner seeks to focus exclusively on a "mantra" that he repeats over and over in his head. The mantra itself is usually a word with no hard consonants and no inherent meaning to the practitioner. ("Ayam" is an example.) What the practitioner usually finds, however, is that his mind repeatedly slips away from the mantra, to focus instead on different thought streams that spring up seemingly on their own. These thoughts usually concern events that recently evoked some response from the practitioner: contentment, pride, joy, but more often feelings like anxiety, worry, or fear. During those more negative thought streams, the practitioner's heart rate might increase and he might literally feel nervous energy coursing through him. But that process—of focusing on the mantra, and then having it displaced by thought streams that are themselves driven by pent-up nervous energy—is a way of dissipating those thoughts and the nervous energy that goes with them. This process—which practitioners call "purification"— might take more or less time during a meditation session, depending on how worked up the practitioner was when he began. George says his "thoughts usually settle out around ten to twelve minutes in." When the process is done, the practitioner feels a serenity, and a stillness, in which solitary insights—intuitions, really—sometimes stand out in stark relief, often before the meditation session is over.

Afterward the practitioner is able to focus on what he wants to focus on, without a lot of background noise. That enhances a leader's ability to analyze problems. "Things seem to be clear when I'm done," George says of his meditation sessions. "Then I grab a piece of paper and start writing down ideas."

PETER CRAWFORD IS something of a solitude renaissance man, in the sense that he uses solitude in a variety of ways. A native of Northern California with degrees from Yale and Stanford Business School, Peter is an alumnus of McKinsey Consulting and now a senior executive at Schwab. "For me solitude brings all kinds of benefits," he says. "Cognitive, emotional, spiritual. Also physical." Growing up, he sought out solitude at "pivotal times. One night in high school I was stressing out about college applications. So I got on my bike and rode out into the Presidio. I rode around for an hour with no lights. I just needed to get away." In college, the summer before his senior year at Yale, when his classmates had internships at Bain and Goldman Sachs, Peter worked as a back-country ranger in Washington State. "I was clearing my head to make decisions about what I'd do after my senior year. I needed that clarity."

As an executive at Schwab, Peter makes solitude part of his daily routine—though he says that "I actually didn't think of it as solitude before you mentioned it." Every morning Peter wakes at five A.M., exercises, and then goes to work early. "The first hour of the day is the best for thinking," he says. "In the morning light my mind is fresh and clear. It's like stripping away all the cookies on a computer. Once they're cleared, my mind works better."

Peter also finds clarity on night runs near his home. His practice is similar to the Buddhist practice of "walking meditation," where, instead of focusing on a mantra, the practitioner seeks to focus exclusively on the physical act of walking—lifting one foot and then the other. Peter runs with a headlamp that allows him to see ten feet ahead. "No music, no headphones," he says. "I go blank. Just focusing on my gait. Just clearing out my mind."

Liza Howard likewise clears her mind on long runs—in her

case, very long runs. Liza is one of the world's elite ultramarathon-
ers, competing and often winning 100-mile races in venues around
the world. (Her fastest time for a 100-miler is 15 hours, 7 minutes—
a 100-mile pace of 9 minutes per mile.) Typically she runs through
the hills of Southwest Texas, on rocky trails with oak and juniper
trees in some places, and cactus and sotol in others.

Liza's description of what running does for her echoes Bill
George's description of what meditation does for him: "It's a distilling process," she says. "The detritus of daily living drops down,
and I'm left with what's important." But the process itself is different: "A good part of your attention is consumed in the physical act.
There's only so much attention left over. That leads to focus."
Retired Marine Corps General James Mattis makes the same
point. "A physically vigorous life is not incompatible with a
contemplative life," he says. "The loss of nervous energy into a
physical act creates a clarity of thinking."

SOLITUDE ALSO FACILITATES structured thinking, which in
turn is essential to analytical clarity. Peter Crawford writes memos
to himself as a way of clarifying his thoughts. "I usually don't
send them to anyone. I'm just collecting my thoughts in a structured way." The practice reaches back to his days at McKinsey.
"They put such a premium on clarity there." His memos follow a
storyline: "Here's the situation—here's the challenge we face—
here's what we should do. It's the McKinsey model of situation,
complication, resolution."

As a husband and father of two children, Peter now engages in
the same practice at home. "I keep a parenting journal," he says.
"Initially, I just wanted to record cute, poignant moments so that
I could remember them later. But I began to realize that I could
use the journal to collect my thoughts as a parent, about troubles
we're having, tough decisions we're facing. Parenting brings
emotional highs and lows, anguish, questioning, second-guessing."
Usually he makes his journal entries late at night. "Sometimes
when I retreat I'm frazzled, spent. But then I collect my thoughts
and come back with a new perspective, more resilient."

Like Peter Crawford, Sarah Dillard uses solitude to gather her thoughts in a structured way. Sarah is an educational entrepreneur, with experience as a senior official in the federal Department of Education. She also played a leading role in the merger of two school districts in Memphis—one comprising mostly black students, the other mostly white—which remains to this day the largest merger of school districts in U.S. history. More recently, she was an executive at Quad Learning, a consulting firm that advises community colleges about how to increase their graduation rates. She now runs SPD Advisory, an education-consulting firm of her own. "For me, there's a difference between my everyday routine of solitude and the big version of it," she says. Her everyday routine begins with a fifteen-minute walk to work in Washington, D.C. "My morning practice is prospective rather than reflective. I'm setting the table for the day, identifying the things I need to work on, the things I need to accomplish." While at work, she keeps open in the background of her computer a document where, on a rolling basis, she records events that trigger an emotional response. "I color-code each entry," she says. "Green means I felt good about it, red means I felt bad. Things that I'd do differently I code in purple." Then, every Wednesday morning, she works at home for a few hours to review her entries without interruptions. "I'm making connections between things in my notes. And I'm reflecting on how we did. What things worked? What didn't? I'm learning about how the team is performing."

Sarah follows the same approach—gathering data, and then reflecting on it—in evaluating the performance of each person she leads. "I do one-on-one meetings with the people who work with me. After each meeting, I record in Google Notes what we talked about during the meeting. Once per quarter I go back and review my notes from my meetings with each person. Sometimes I'll connect things I hadn't seen before. Or I'll notice progress. Or I'll realize things I've done wrong, things I should apologize for."

Sarah makes a point to reflect at a company-wide level as well. "I can't imagine how someone doing a start-up wouldn't do reflection," she says. "In a start-up you have to learn fast, or it's not going to work. Reflection is the key way to learn. You have open loops of things you're doing for the first time. If you're just caught up in what's happening, if you don't reflect, you're not closing those loops. You're not learning the best way to do those things." She also says that "in a start-up you're going to encounter 'unknown unknowns.' You need to process and learn from those. Otherwise you won't be clear about what happened."

NATE FICK USES time alone for both analysis and intuition. "You have to structure in time for solitude," says Fick, author of the bestselling memoir *One Bullet Away*. "Otherwise you're just reacting to other people's thoughts, rather than driving the direction yourself."

Fick is a former Marine Recon officer, having served in the invasions of Afghanistan in 2001 and Iraq in 2003. He later served as the president of the Center for a New American Security, an influential national-security think tank in Washington. He is now the CEO of Endgame Inc., a firm specializing in cyber-threat defenses. "I tell my assistant I need ninety minutes a day on my calendar to close the door and think," he says. The same goes for the people who work for him: "I tell my subordinates that two days each month, no one has any meetings. Otherwise the days get so hectic that you have no time to process or to think. The only way to combat it, short of what Thoreau did, is structurally to build in the space."

Fick finds ways to resist today's norm of constant connectivity. "At some point the inputs become intrusions," he says. "I used to have this phone that had a blinking light on it in my office at home. I would get frustrated to have that light blinking at me whenever I had a message on there. So I threw it out and bought a 1970s rotary phone. No voicemail, no flashing light on there. It's been a marked improvement." He also seeks solitude outdoors. "I sail on Chesapeake Bay," he says. His sailboat is "big enough to take the family, but small enough to single-sail. The boat would be worthless to me if I couldn't single-sail it."

Fick accesses intuition during time alone. "That's when stuff percolating in the subconscious crystallizes and takes form." The process often occurs during a run, which for Fick can stretch ninety minutes or more. "I often start a run thinking, 'Here's what I need to figure out.' So I start thinking about that, and then after two minutes I'm off onto something else. But almost inevitably, by the time I'm done running, I'll have circled back and finished my thinking about that issue. It was percolating the whole time."

Peter Crawford describes the same phenomenon during his runs. "Usually, what happens is that there is something that I'm struggling with—a strategic question, a presentation that I'm supposed to make, a conversation that I need to have, an organizational decision that I need to make. I don't consciously think about it when I'm running, but an idea or the answer will suddenly pop into my head—either as I'm running or quite often soon after I finish. Things get cleared out in my head, so either the idea finds its way to the surface or the mechanics of my brain work better and are more easily able to process the problem in the background."

RETIRED U.S. ARMY four-star General Stanley McChrystal likewise relies on solitude to access intuition. General McChrystal served as commander of U.S. forces in Afghanistan during 2009–10 and commander of the U.S. Joint Special Operations Command during 2003–06, among many other positions. He is the author of *My Share of the Task*, an autobiography, and the coauthor of *Team of Teams*, a leadership book. He is also the cofounder of the McChrystal Group, a consulting firm in Alexandria, Virginia. "Solitude to me just means the chance to think," he says. "It doesn't need to be a quiet place. It just has to be in a place where I can allow my mind to focus on something." While deployed in the Middle East, he often found solitude in the air. "Helicopter rides were good for thinking about decisions. I'd put the headphones on. No one can mess with you. Not getting e-mails. Just watching the brown terrain passing by below, hour after hour. I felt centered." He also finds solitude while working out. "I don't run with anyone, I don't work out with anyone."

General McChrystal observes, "Technology has brought changes to leadership. The barrier to entry to contact leaders is so low now, with e-mail. I don't want to be rude to people. And responding to emails can make you feel like you're getting a lot done. But when you're doing that you're not taking time to think."

He considers himself "lousy at assessing people on first impression. I have to let my intuition work before I can do that. It takes a little bit of time." His process for making leadership decisions is similar. "Sometimes I have to think about a problem in several steps. Solitude lets me play that out. It lets me remind myself about what's important." Intuition tells General McChrystal whether a decision fits the pattern of his values. "I do benefit from hearing other people's thoughts. I might have an initial reaction, but my values might not always govern my initial response. It's better if I don't make the decision then. It's better to marinate in that information and make the decision later," he says. "If I spend some time in solitude thinking about it, I find that I circle back to my values.

"When I was a regimental commander, before the wars, we came up with a plan after working all night," he recalls. "We were invested in it. All the staff analysis had been done. Then I slept for a few hours, woke up, and realized the plan was crap. I had provided the guidance, and the analysis went from there. But my intuition told me it was wrong."

His experience illustrates that intuition requires a degree of mental quietude. "In the moment, I'm responding to stimuli," he says. "Later, my values reassert themselves through intuition. And if the analysis or recommendation doesn't feel right, I go with my intuition. Solitude brings that out."

HOWARD PRINCE HAS used intuition under the most harrowing of circumstances. Today he is one of the nation's preeminent scholars on leadership, holding the Lloyd Hackler Endowed Chair in Ethical Leadership at the University of Texas at Austin, and having earlier served as the founding dean of the University of Richmond's Jepson School of Leadership Studies. Before that, as an Army officer, Prince earned a Ph.D. in psychology and founded the Department of Behavioral Sciences and Leadership at West Point. He retired from the Army in 1990, as a brigadier general, after twenty-eight years of active duty. Prince says that "leadership is about consensual interdependence. The leader chooses to depend on his followers, and the followers choose to depend on the leader. That means, even in the military, you can't just command people. Leaders have to transform themselves from being just a commander or boss to a *leader*. A leader interacts with his followers, gets them to believe that this person is worth following, that he's going someplace and I want to go there too." Prince says that the "stereotyping of leaders" creates a bias against solitude. "Solitude can give you silver bullets as a leader. But there's this idea that leaders have to be flaming extroverts. There's also an action bias: 'Do something!' Sometimes it's more important to stop and get your wits together."

Prince did exactly that on February 20, 1968, when he was an army captain and company commander during the Tet Offensive in Vietnam. Three weeks before, the North Vietnamese Army (NVA) had broken a cease-fire agreement during the Vietnamese high holiday of Tet to invade the historic city of Hue, in South Vietnam. Since then the U.S. Marines had been engaged in intense door-to-door combat to retake the city. Prince was a member of an Army "air cavalry" battalion (the "air cav" troopers typically moved from place to place in UH-1 "Huey" helicopters), which at the beginning of February was located about ten miles northwest of Hue. The battalion comprised four companies of about 125 men apiece. Prince commanded B Company. Prince's battalion commander was Lieutenant Colonel Jim Vaught, a brawny South Carolinian who had fought as a private in World War II and as a lieutenant in Korea. Vaught had taken command of Prince's battalion only a few days before, after his predecessor was killed in an NVA rocket attack. Prince remembers Vaught as a first-rate leader. "He shared his men's burdens and created a culture of truth. Vaught dug his own foxholes, and taught us how to dig them. When we got shot at, he got shot at. And he'd never leave the battlefield until all the wounded got evacuated first."

As for the point about truth, Prince recalls his first meeting with Vaught. "He arrived early in the morning, with his full battle gear on. He walked up to me to introduce himself and said, 'I'm scared shitless, and I presume you are too. Now that we have that out of the way, let's figure out what to do.'" A few days later, after the battalion's first battle with the NVA outside Hue, Prince's radio operator was talking with brigade headquarters, negotiating a body count, which was the number of enemy soldiers purportedly killed in an engagement. "The body count was an obscene metric," Prince says. "We had no idea how many of their guys we'd killed. They took care of their dead and wounded just like we did. When Vaught heard my operator negotiating the body count, he strode over, grabbed the handset, and yelled into it, 'WE DON'T HAVE A BODY COUNT! OUT!!' That was a critical leadership action. He was creating a culture of truth."

On February 5, Vaught's battalion received orders to move by foot toward Hue. "We made contact the first day," Prince says. "The NVA shot down a Huey helicopter. Vaught sent me over to find the crew. We didn't find them and never knew what happened to them." By February 7, the battalion had reached Thon La Chu, about four miles northwest of Hue. There the NVA shot down another Huey next to a woodline. Vaught's battalion took a position inside the woods, known as Thon Lieu Coc Thuong. The woods were "all primary growth, fairly new trees," Prince says. "Not a real barrier to movement." Three hundred meters to the southeast, across open, dry rice paddies ("it was the dry season, they weren't growing then") was another wooded area, known as Thon Que Chu. From an observation post at the edge of Thon Lieu, the Americans saw intense NVA activity around a large concrete bunker in Thon Que. "We had no idea how many of them were out there, but it turned out to be a very large force," Prince says.

The next day, February 8, Vaught ordered Prince's company to conduct a reconnaissance-in-force across the rice paddies toward Thon Que. "The rice paddies were wide open. No cover or conceal-ment," Prince says. At about one P.M. his men set out toward Thon Que in single file, the way they had always moved when fighting in the jungle. Nothing happened as they crossed the field. Then, just as the troopers entered the woods at Thon Que, they were ambushed from three sides, dropping every man in the lead squad.

Unbeknownst to any of Vaught's men, an entire NVA regiment was dug in there. Vaught's battalion was outnumbered five to one, and Prince's men were hopelessly outnumbered. It took three hours of intense fighting for Prince's men to disengage the NVA and retreat back to Thon Lieu.

Four days later, on February 12, the battalion's other three companies attacked Thon Que, with Prince's company in reserve. "They were repulsed. They couldn't break in." Meanwhile, the Americans and the NVA exchanged mortar fire day and night. "It felt like we were constantly under attack," Prince says. Thirteen of Prince's men were hit by mortar fire in a single afternoon. By February 20, every officer in Prince's company—other than Prince and a second lieutenant who had been in Vietnam only two weeks—had been killed or wounded.

On the afternoon of February 20, Vaught brought his company commanders together to brief them on an attack planned for the next day. "Our orders are to take the NVA position—at all costs," Vaught told them. The battalion second-in-command, Major Charlie Baker, had drawn up the plan for the attack after flying above the NVA position in a small spotter plane. The plan was complex: three of the battalion's companies would attack the NVA's position from different directions, with Prince's company— now depleted 50 percent by casualties—in the lead. Moreover, rather than cross the rice paddies in single file, Prince's men would move abreast, with two platoons stretched out in front, and two companies behind them putting out suppressive fire at the NVA. Then the platoons in the rear would leapfrog the ones in front, which would put out suppressive fire, and so on. Once Vaught's men entered the woods, three other American battalions would move in to support them.

Prince brought his four platoon leaders together that evening to brief them on the plan. One was the green lieutenant; the others were sergeants, because the lieutenants formerly in command of their platoons had been wounded or killed. Prince explained the movement they would make the next morning and dismissed them. By then it was early evening.

A short while later, the lieutenant came back.

"Sir, they won't go," he said.

"What do you mean they won't go?" Prince asked.

"They just won't go."

Speaking about it now, Prince says, "I vividly remember thinking, 'What do you mean they won't go?? The plan is tactically sound! It's not unethical!'" Prince sent the lieutenant away. "I got really, really angry. But I was really experiencing fear, and it manifested as anger. I wanted to run over there and chew their ass. But for some reason, I controlled that."

At that moment Prince faced a supreme crisis of leadership. "Deep inside, part of me asked, 'What are you going to do now, Captain?' Nothing in my training or experience told me what to do." He also faced two impediments to clear thinking. The first was emotional interference: no one as angry and scared as Prince was in those first moments can think clearly. The other was fragmentary information: he truly had no idea why the men in the lieutenant's platoon were refusing to go.

Rather than take action right away, Prince chose to take some time alone. "I stomped around in the woods by myself for about a half hour. Just inside our perimeter, with darkness setting in. Trying to gather my thoughts." Prince's efforts to analyze the problem got nowhere. "I simply could not understand their response. I'd think of one possible reason for it, then another. None made sense." Eventually his anger began to dissipate somewhat. Then Prince tried a different approach. "I just let things percolate. Let myself free-think." Finally, in that relative quietude, an intuition surfaced. "I needed to talk to them. *Really* talk to them. Not yell. But I still didn't know what I'd do when I went over there."

Prince walked over to the lieutenant's platoon. All the men, the lieutenant included, were looking down. "No one would make eye contact with me."

Prince said, "Hey, guys, what's going on?"

For a while nobody answered. Then one of the enlisted men said, "Sir, we think you're going to get us all killed tomorrow so you can get a medal."

Prince was stunned. "What do you mean?"

"Sir, we've never done it this way before."

Prince recalls, "Then it clicked. I knew what to do." Part of effective leadership is knowing your audience, and at this moment Prince knew his. "They were used to looking for the enemy in thick vegetation, in single file. Everyone but the point man felt relatively safe, and we rotated the point man every thirty minutes. They had no tactical training for what we were going to do the next day." The idea of moving abreast across wide-open rice-paddy fields made the men feel like they'd all be walking on point toward the NVA position. "I squatted down and sketched out in the dirt the tactics we'd be using. Moving in single file is why we'd gotten ambushed on February 8. I explained to them that the way we were going to do it tomorrow was the best way, really the only way, to attack the NVA position."

The men stood there listening, watching Prince sketch out the plan in the dirt. Some of the men glanced at each other. Finally one of them spoke for the group.

"Okay, we'll do it."

Prince had met the challenge before him, and the next day his men helped take the NVA position. (Prince himself was almost fatally wounded in the attack and spent seven months in a U.S. hospital afterward.) "It goes back to consensual interdependence," Prince says. "The problem was the information they didn't have. I needed to lead them, not command them." Sometimes in Vietnam, if the men thought an officer was getting his men killed because of incompetence or ambition, the officer would get "fragged": someone would roll a live grenade into his tent in the middle of the night. Prince says, "If I had gone over and yelled at them and used command authority, I'm convinced I would've been fragged during the night before the attack."

A LEADER SHOULD strive for clarity not only about the challenges he faces but about himself, his strengths and weaknesses as a leader. Nate Fick sees "a distinction between self-awareness and self-consciousness." The latter Fick sees as something to be wary of: a mindset that is focused outward, which can lead to posturing and decisions based on how others will perceive them. But self-awareness, in Fick's view, is something to develop: an understanding of the forces within oneself that cause one to do or feel certain things as a leader. The mindset is fundamentally introspective. The understanding that it brings usually comes only after sustained and searching thought. And thus, Fick says, "I think solitude is essential to self-awareness."

One way to gain self-awareness is through physical adversity. "Suffering throws open the doors," says Liza Howard, the ultra-marathoner. "Physical suffering strips you down to the bare fundamentals. It humbles you. You can't hide from it. You have to decide who you are and what you're going to do." Peter Crawford's experience is similar. "I grew up hiking in the mountains," he says. "Hiking up there strips away all the ornamentation of everyday life. When you strip down to the fundamentals is when you reveal character, and forge it."

Another way to obtain self-awareness is through reflection. Bill George teaches graduate students at Harvard Business School "to process your life story. You need to reflect on the crucibles of your life and how you dealt with them. Those experiences can teach you about your character, and things you can try to improve."

Nate Fick has practiced what George teaches. Fick contrasts his two trips back to the United States after his deployments to Iraq and Afghanistan. "After Iraq, we took a plane home. We went from Iraq to L.A. in seventy-two hours. We didn't have time to process the change. It made the adjustment harder." But the trip home from Afghanistan was different. "We had been deployed there on a ship, and we left on a ship. The ship was small, with a small flight pad on the stern for helicopters. There were a thousand guys on board. But the ship had a big superstructure, and we could go outside all the time. I spent two to three hours a day, usually alone, leaning on the rail. You were fifty to seventy feet above the water and could see to the horizon in every direction. Looking at where the sea meets the sky all around. We were a thousand miles from land. At night the stars were spectacular. That trip home was recharging, energizing."

FICK'S DESCRIPTION OF his seaborne journey reaches over to the spiritual side of leadership, where a leader disconnects from the Lilliputian inputs of daily life to connect with some transcendent purpose or meaning. Sometimes that connection is a sense of unity with nature's grandeur. Peter Crawford finds that kind of connection during two-hour trail runs on Mount Tamalpais, on the Pacific Coast near San Francisco. "I lose myself in that moment," Peter says. "I become part of that landscape. It's primal, down to the essence of what we were thousands of years ago." Peter finds that same connection during solo backpacking trips in the mountains each year. "I love the awesomeness of the mountains," he says. There, surrounded only by sublimity, "you're a part of this much, much grander thing than yourself. You feel close to God. I'm not incredibly religious, but I feel this hunger, a craving for that. I can feel tired, burned out, frustrated—but after two days in the mountains I come back refreshed."

Sarah Dillard uses what she calls the "big version" of solitude to reconnect with her core values. "I make my best decisions in nature," she says. "In the city, there's a lot of energy, but also a lot of inputs that pull you away from your center. Things like ambition, achievement, the impression you're making around you." Those are things that can make a person externally motivated, measuring success by what others think. "Being in nature keeps me internally motivated," she says. "It's humbling. It brings me back to my center."

She describes an example of this kind of solitude. "I was working on a start-up with a partner. We were in the process of creating it. Then he bailed. I had to decide whether to go forward alone. So I booked a one-way ticket to Colorado and stayed in a cabin in the Flatirons mountains, above Boulder. That was a pretty acute version of solitude." There, she worked in the cabin each morning and then hiked a half-dozen miles in the Flatirons each afternoon. "There were fewer stimuli once I was in Colorado. But it wasn't just about turning down the outside noise. The effect was cognitive, emotional, and spiritual. I get from the mountains what other people get from church. You can measure their duration in geologic time. It gave me perspective." She realized eventually that "this project I thought I was founding was never going to materialize. The situation was never going to feel like a success. It felt messy when I was in it. It felt messy when I was coming out of it." But while hiking in the Flatirons, "I was clear about what I was going to do."

SUSAN CAIN USES solitude to identify the larger purposes behind her leadership. Susan is the author of the runaway bestseller *Quiet: The Power of Introverts in a World That Can't Stop Talking*. More recently she founded the Quiet Revolution, which teaches organizations around the world how to perform better by allowing their introverted employees to follow their reflective nature. As a strong introvert herself, however, Susan sometimes finds her new role as a high-profile leader to be draining. "I never feel like solitude is something I do consciously," she says. "I just naturally do it to seek a state of homeostasis." Susan observes that "introverts usually don't want to be leaders just for the sake of being a leader. The status, the attention, aren't things that most introverts put a lot of value on. When introverts are leaders, it's usually because the work they're doing is really important to them." She cites her work at the Quiet Revolution as an example. "We've started a program called the Quiet Ambassadors. They're people who are passionate about our message, who are trained in substance and methodology to take our ideas about the power of introverts across the country. The impact we're having on organizations and individuals is what gets me excited about what I'm doing."

Liza Howard found a sense of purpose during a long run in May 2011, when she listened to a podcast that featured another ultramarathoner, Mike Erwin, talking about his then-new organization, Team Red, White & Blue. Team RWB's mission is to connect veterans to their communities through physical and social activity. Mike's comments gave Liza the idea of founding a trail-running

camp for veterans. Back then Liza and her husband had just moved
to San Antonio. "It's a big city, without a big outdoor community.
I felt very alone. I didn't have many friends." A trail-running camp
under the auspices of Team RWB "could bring everyone together,"
she thought. "There's a tradition in long-distance trail running
where older, more experienced trail runners pass down their
knowledge to the newer ones. The elders tell the new runners about
what's going to happen on long runs, what they can expect." A
running camp for veterans "could bring them into our community, and create friendships."

But implementing the idea would be complicated. "We had no
idea who would come, or what their abilities would be. We needed
to figure out how to accommodate people with different levels of
fitness. Some people can't run far. But we didn't want to hold the
other people back. We'd also have to figure out how much we
could teach people in one weekend." Over a series of long runs of
her own, Liza worked out the answers to those questions and
others. "I was trying to reach a clarity of vision," she says.

Today her vision is a reality, in the form of Camp Eagle in
Rocksprings, Texas. "It's an old church camp, in hill country," she
says. "The nearest town is forty-five minutes away. There's no
phone service, and there's Internet only in an inconvenient location." Campers are divided into four groups, "based on fitness and
skill," she says. "They sleep in old dorm rooms, twelve to a room,
and we all eat in a large dining room." The camp operates one
weekend each year, in October, from Friday afternoon through
noon Monday. Typically about fifty veterans attend, all for free,
joined by a few dozen civilians who pay a fee and a few dozen more
volunteers. The volunteer instructors—called mentors—are all
elite trail runners. "We send out invites to mentors each year. No
one has ever turned it down." Camp participants learn about tech-
nical running form, trail etiquette, first aid, injury prevention,
nutrition, and heat and hydration management—all things that
Liza worked out during her runs. Yet the more important benefits
transcend the running itself. On the one hand, the camp shows
participants a way to experience solitude for themselves. But on the

other, "the participants make a connection with each other, and with the mentors. They become part of a community," she says, echoing Team RWB's mission. "They're really happy and excited when they leave."

ALTHOUGH HE WOULD never say it himself, Tommy Caldwell is probably the best "free climber" in the world. In free climbing, one climbs up some rock surface—usually a cliff—using one's hands and feet, searching out crevices and rocky protrusions to grab onto or push off from. The climber is harnessed to a rope only to catch him if he falls. Now age thirty-seven, Caldwell won his first national climbing championship when he was sixteen. Solitude is a central part of his life. "It's the quiet moments for me when the pieces of life knit themselves together," he says.

Solitude connects Tommy with his core values. One of them is a strong sense of empathy. "Solitude softens my heart," he says. That same centering effect draws Tommy to solitude during pivotal moments in his life. "All the most important decisions in my life have come in moments of solitude. So if I'm up against a big decision, I create those moments." he says. "I remember the moment when I decided to become a big-wall climber. It was during a seventeen-hour drive. I didn't begin that drive thinking I'd be a big-wall climber. But by the end I was."

One episode of solitude came not by choice. When Tommy was twenty-one, as his climbing career was starting to take off, he cut off his left index finger in an accident with a table saw. The injury was career-threatening: a climber is constantly using his fingers, especially an index finger, to pull himself up. "The doctors reattached it, and then tried to keep it alive. But over the next few days it just turned black." Finally his doctor told Tommy that they needed to remove the finger—and that he would not be able to climb again. "I was devastated," he says. "Over the next four days in the hospital, I reflected back on my life. As a kid I was a squirt with bad hand-eye coordination. Climbing was the first thing that felt right in my life. I thought I might not find my way in life again." But then determination set in. "Those days of reflection made me realize how much climbing meant to me. I felt a conviction to continue climbing. It was blind faith. I chose not to think about it beyond that." Five months later, Tommy free-climbed the 3,000-foot Salathe Face on El Capitan in Yosemite National Park.

In the years that followed, Tommy climbed all the different faces on El Capitan, save one—the Dawn Wall, whose smooth, nearly vertical granite surface was thought to be impossible to free-climb. But in late 2007, after a painful divorce, Tommy began thinking about climbing it. "There was a void in my life then. The idea of climbing the Dawn Wall was a coping mechanism, a goal for me to work toward." Tommy made his first attempt to climb the Dawn Wall in 2010, joined by Kevin Jorgeson, a strong but less-experienced climber. They failed. Over the next four years, the pair made four more attempts. Each time they failed.

They tried once more, starting on December 27, 2014. By then their efforts had gained attention nationwide, and a sizable press contingent was present to cover the attempt. As in their other attempts, the pair divided the 3,000-foot face into thirty-two "pitches." The goal was to climb all thirty-two pitches without returning to the ground. If a climber fell during a pitch—which involved a 50-foot drop until the rope caught him—he had to start the pitch again from the beginning. During the day they would climb pitches when conditions permitted. At night they slept on 6-foot by 4-foot "portaledges," 2,000 feet up, suspended by nylon straps and hanging from bolts in the sheer granite wall. Each day a climbing friend ascended 1,200 feet up a rope to deliver water and supplies, with Tommy or Kevin rappelling down to meet him.

The climb began well: in their first six days of climbing, each climber successfully climbed the first fourteen pitches. On their prior attempts they had never gotten above pitch 12. But even though he and Kevin were climbing well, Tommy felt they were not meeting their goals. "It was a media circus around us up there." Cameramen suspended from the summit recorded the climbers' every move. Even more problematic, Tommy and Kevin had full cell and Internet service on El Capitan, so Tommy felt obligated to tweet reports of his progress each day. He despised it. "I was really frustrated that we'd become so distracted with our phones," he says. The year before, Tommy had climbed with another friend for five days in Patagonia, without cell service. "Alex and I were incredibly bonded during that climb," he said. "I wondered why the same thing wasn't happening now. It was because we were distracted. We weren't thinking about what the climb meant."

Then Kevin ran into serious trouble. Over the next seven days, while Tommy successfully climbed pitches 15–20, Kevin fell ten times while trying to climb pitch 15. "I was doing everything I could to help Kevin, during the day when we climbed, at night talking about it on the ledge." Then, after the sixth day of Kevin's attempts to climb pitch 15, mishap became metaphor. "I came back to our ledge that night," Tommy says. "Kevin had just finished a devastating series of attempts. I put my phone in my chest pocket and was clipping stuff onto a rope, feeling devastated for Kevin. I leaned over to pick something up. Then it happened: the phone fell out of my pocket, down two thousand feet, and smashed apart on the rocks below." He had forgotten to zip the pocket. Tommy's first reaction was "Oh, no." But then he thought, "This is the best thing ever! Now I can stay focused on this extraordinary experience."

Two days later, on January 9, Kevin successfully climbed pitch 15. From there both climbers surged upward with new energy. "Without the phone, I was able to sit and contemplate," he says. "Each day there are only a handful of hours that are good for climbing. When I wasn't climbing, I sat there looking out at the mountains from two thousand feet up. Reflecting on what the climb meant. Solitude is such a powerful force. It's spiritual to me."

Five days later, both climbers climbed pitch 32 and reached the summit. "Reflecting up there on the ledge, I realized that the relationships are more important than reaching the summit," Tommy says. "The journey, the relationships. That's the beauty of the climb."

CHAPTER 2

Analytical Clarity
Dwight D. Eisenhower, 1944

"Make big decisions in the calm."
—DWIGHT D. EISENHOWER

The hardest-earned kind of clarity is analytical clarity. Unlike intuitive clarity—which arises more from mental quietude than from strenuous effort—analytical clarity arises from rigorous syllogistic thought. And that kind of thinking—because of its difficulty, and its glacial pace—is best done, and perhaps only done, in solitude.

The process is one of breaking down complexity to a single point of decision. The leader must first identify, as clearly and precisely as he can, the goal he seeks to achieve or the problem he seeks to solve. Sometimes that identification is easy, as for a judge who must decide whether the evidence at trial was sufficient to support a defendant's conviction for a particular crime. Other times—as for one family member troubled by the behavior of another—specifically identifying the problem might begin the process of finding a solution to it.

Typically, in situations calling for analytical clarity, the leader confronts a complex and often jumbled mass of information. The leader must sort that information logically: for a corporate leader, for example, some data might pertain to changes in technology;

other data might pertain to competitors' products; still other data might pertain to generational preferences among consumers. Then, having brought some logical order to the information itself, the leader must develop from it a series of logical premises. Those premises typically begin with certain facts that are known or likely to exist. The premises then proceed to include certain rules or principles—the product must be produced for a certain cost, or it must be launched by a certain date, or a certain legal standard must be met—with which the leader's decision must comply. This stage of the process often reveals that some information, which at first seemed important, is in fact immaterial: it does not affect compliance with a governing rule or principle, and thus cannot affect the decision either way. After this process of sorting and then sifting information, the leader is left with a series of premises— about facts and governing standards—about which she is often quite confident.

The harder question usually concerns how those facts and standards intersect. Sometimes (as in, say, legal reasoning) the relevant facts are known; the real question is what, exactly, the governing standard means. But more often some of the relevant facts remain unknown—because the leader's information is fragmentary, or the relevant events have not happened yet.

In either instance, the object of the exercise is the same: identification of the key variable upon which the leader's decision depends. That variable, depending on which way it breaks, is the one that determines whether the benefits of a particular leadership decision exceed its costs. Identification of that variable is what provides analytical clarity: what began as a mass of undifferentiated information is now a landscape of logical premises that lead to one critical point. As to more difficult leadership decisions, therefore, analytical clarity does not always allow the leader to know which decision is best. But it does allow the leader to focus, clearly and specifically, on the key variable that will determine whether a decision brings success or failure. The leader can then determine—sometimes based on focused analysis of the variable itself, other times based on gut instinct (which is to say intuition)—which way he thinks the variable will break. And from that determination the leader's decision follows.

Dwight D. Eisenhower engaged in this process throughout World War II. That was most notably true in June 1944—when responsibility for the success or failure of the D-day invasion rested on his shoulders alone, and the critical variable, out of all the massive complexity then facing him, was simple: the weather.

DWIGHT EISENHOWER WAS the most extroverted of leaders. Perpetually upbeat, with a wide, infectious grin, Eisenhower was, by his own description, "a born optimist." Always energetic, he became even more so around people, his hands and facial features continually animated, his pronouncements crisp and decisive. A reporter observed him "walking up and down, pacing patterns on the rug, his flat, harsh voice ejecting idea after idea like sparks flung from an emery wheel." But unlike Douglas MacArthur— under whom Eisenhower served for seven years after the First World War, and who was more a negative example for Eisenhower than a positive one—Eisenhower was not dictatorial. Instead, throughout his tenure as commander of Allied forces in North Africa and then Europe, Eisenhower was humble, earnestly engaging the people around him, seeking compromise wherever he could. His sincerity was universally recognized; so was his reputation for fair dealing. The overall effect was to energize others as much as they energized him. Even his most prickly lieutenant, British Field Marshal Bernard Montgomery, wrote that Eisenhower drew "the hearts of men towards him as a magnet draws the bits of metal." Montgomery wrote further, in his diary shortly before D-day: "He has a generous and lovable character, and I would trust him to the last gasp."

Yet even Eisenhower—the most sociable of men—deliberately sought out solitude at the most critical junctures of his leadership. The practice reached back to the very outset of the war. Just five days after Pearl Harbor, then serving as a one-star general in San Antonio, Eisenhower received orders to report immediately to the War Department. Eisenhower had no idea why he was summoned but took the next plane to Washington. Upon arriving, Eisenhower was promptly ushered into a meeting alone with Army Chief of Staff George C. Marshall. Without preamble, for the next twenty minutes Marshall outlined the United States' calamitous position in the Pacific. The fleet in Pearl Harbor would be disabled for months. The Japanese had also bombed the Philippines, inflicting unknown but presumably severe damage upon the American aircraft there. The American garrison in the Philippines was tiny, and the Filipino ground forces inadequately trained. And the Japanese meant to overrun the islands as soon as possible.

Then Marshall looked Eisenhower in the eye and abruptly asked: "What should be our general line of action?" Eisenhower hesitated for a moment—he had not even unpacked his bag yet—but he had the presence of mind not to answer off the cuff. He asked for "a few hours" to think about it. Marshall agreed.

Eisenhower then retreated to a vacant office to prepare the first of many memoranda distilling his thoughts during the war. As he sat there, Eisenhower wrote later, "a curious echo from the long ago came to my aid." He thought back to his time with General Fox Conner, his mentor during World War I, a man he admired above all others. Conner had told Eisenhower again and again that another great war would come, and that when it did come, the one man who could lead the American military was "Marshall—he is close to being a genius." With Conner's description of Marshall in mind, Eisenhower resolved "that my answer should be short, emphatic, and based on reasoning in which I honestly believed." In his memorandum—entitled "Steps to Be Taken"—Eisenhower asserted that, even though the Filipino cause appeared hopeless, the United States should send an aircraft carrier from San Diego to Australia, build up a strong base of supply there, and make every effort to save the Philippines. The problem, as Eisenhower saw it, was not strictly military. His thoughts reflected the broader political perspective that would prove essential to his leadership throughout the war. Handing the memo to Marshall, Eisenhower said, "We must do everything for them that is humanly possible. The people of China, of the Philippines, of the Dutch East Indies will be watching us. They may excuse failure but they will not excuse abandonment."

Marshall quietly replied, "I agree with you. Do your best to save them."

That proved to be the first of many analytical challenges that Eisenhower faced during the war. In 1942, Eisenhower confronted grave and to some extent insuperable logistical problems as he coordinated, from Washington, relief efforts for the Philippines. And later, as commander of Allied forces in North Africa in 1942 and in Italy in 1943, and above all as Supreme Commander of the Allied invasion of France in 1944, Eisenhower confronted leadership questions of the utmost complexity. Those challenges went far beyond engaging and defeating the enemy. They included the creation of a military force large and well-trained enough to confront the triumphant Germans; the maintenance of supply lines across oceans patrolled by German submarines; and the always-delicate process of coordination with America's British and, to a lesser extent, Free French allies. These issues presented Eisenhower with a staggering amount of information to sort, synthesize, and then act upon. But before Eisenhower could act— before he could lead the legions of men beneath him—he had to achieve clarity in his own mind. And in that process, from Eisenhower's first meeting with Marshall to the end of the war, solitude played an essential role.

For Eisenhower, the most rigorous way to think about a subject was to write about it. And so, on the subjects most important to his work, he made a practice of writing to himself. His son John— himself a West Point graduate who spent weeks by his father's side during the Normandy campaign—wrote after the war that "throughout his life my father had put many of his thoughts on paper, partly for the information of others but even more to clarify thoughts in his own mind." That practice had special urgency during the war. In a remarkable February 1943 letter to his wife, Mamie—written just as German General Erwin Rommel began an attack that would rout Eisenhower's forces at Kasserine Pass in Tunisia—Eisenhower wrote about the "loneliness" of leadership, saying that "subordinates can advise, urge, help, and pray—but only one man, in his mind and heart, can decide, 'Do we, or do we not?'" He added: "the strain comes from not being sure that the analysis has been carefully and accurately made."

Eisenhower always strove to make sure, before committing his troops to combat, that the analysis had been "carefully and accurately made." But it was by no means easy for him to find the time to do so. Early in the war he complained about the constant meetings he was forced to attend: "Talk-talk-talk." Later, while stationed in London, he wrote in a letter to Mamie: "This is the longest stretch I've had for writing in a long time. One or two staff officers have been in for a moment since I began the first page, but no real *conferences*. I'm getting to hate the sound of that word." He added: "I've gotten so hard boiled about turning down invitations that I don't even see most of them." In another letter, he told Mamie that "my days are always full. Even when I think I have a couple of hours to myself, something always happens to upset my plans. But it's right that we should be busy—as long as we can retain time to think." Another letter sounded the same theme: "My hours in the office are quite crowded, and necessary journeys are always interrupting. The result is that I must take a few hours off, to think quietly, when I can." And another: "When I get driven to a certain point my natural reaction is to scribble something to you. Sometimes it helps clarify things in my mind."

Eisenhower found time to think and write because he made doing so a priority. His war papers are replete with documents and notes that he wrote not for any official purpose, but specifically to distill his own thoughts. In July 1942, for example, the British rejected an American plan to land Allied forces that fall in Cherbourg, France. The plan was admittedly desperate but was meant to provide emergency assistance to the Russians, whose position then was desperate too. (The Battle of Stalingrad would soon begin.) In a memo for his private diary, Eisenhower concisely described "the far-reaching import" of the British rejection of the plan—that the Allies could do virtually "nothing to help the Russians remain in the war," and that the Allies must improve "our own defensive situation in anticipation of a Russian collapse." Then Eisenhower sketched out the Allies' only remaining option for offensive action, namely an invasion of North Africa, which in fact took place in November 1942—with Eisenhower in command.

A month after the Allied landings in North Africa—code-named Torch—Eisenhower wrote a long and reflective diary entry in which he described the problems facing him in Tunisia and then observed: "An orderly, logical mind" is "absolutely essential" to a leader's success. To that end, Eisenhower dictated another diary entry a week later, in which he catalogued in careful detail the Allied forces in North Africa, the German forces opposing them, and the risks he then faced. The entry lay in Eisenhower's desk for two weeks afterward. When Eisenhower's close friend and senior aide, Harry Butcher, asked him why he had written it, Ike replied: "To crystallize my thoughts." On other occasions Eisenhower identified questions rather than answers. After a 1942 meeting regarding the shortage of Allied landing craft for amphibious invasions—a problem that would plague him throughout the war—Eisenhower wrote out in his notepad five questions that needed answers, among them "How in hell can we win this war unless we crack some heads?" And in August 1943 Eisenhower wrote out five more questions that needed answers regarding the upcoming Allied invasion of Italy. On still other occasions, Eisenhower reduced a day's work to a single exhortation or insight: "We must get going!" or "We have got to have ships!"

Frequently Eisenhower's practice of thinking by writing not only clarified his thoughts, but also stabilized him emotionally. Some of Eisenhower's most difficult moments during the war came in the hours after a major operation began, when success or failure was out of his hands and an infantry lieutenant could do more to affect the outcome than Eisenhower could. His first such moment came on November 8, 1942, during the Torch landings in North Africa, then the largest amphibious invasion ever attempted. Eisenhower waited for news on the island of Gibraltar, in a dank, rat-infested catacomb of limestone tunnels beneath a rocky peak called Mount Misery. There, in a tiny office with a single bulb hanging from the ceiling, Eisenhower wrote out on a sheet of note-paper a ten-point memo entitled "Worries of a Commander." The first was "Spain is so ominously quiet." The third was that, according to early reports, resistance by Vichy French troops "has blazed up." Three other worries involved Henri Giraud, a French general who the Allies hoped could convince the Vichy French to stop fighting, and with whom Eisenhower was engaged in frustrating negotiations. (Giraud demanded that he command all Allied forces in North Africa.) Another was that "we don't know whereabouts or condition of our airborne force." And the last worry: "We cannot find out anything."

Two months later, at his headquarters in Tunisia, Eisenhower wrote another memo for his diary and stuck it in his desk. Again he explained to Butcher that he had written the memo to "clarify his thoughts." But the memo's opening lines state an additional purpose: "The past week has been a succession of disappointments. I'm just writing them down so as to forget them." Eisenhower then blew off steam on several points: "Each day the tactical situation has gotten worse"; "the aggressive action and local attack I had so laboriously planned for 24th and following days have had to be abandoned"; and "the newspapers want my scalp for 'political censorship'—but there is *none*. Has not been for two weeks. Why the yell?"

Sometimes Eisenhower used solitude simply to reflect on the "terribly sad" nature of his work. The night before a battle in North Africa, he silently watched an infantry captain address his men. Eisenhower later described the scene:

> There was no outward stamp of piety on this officer but his words moved me as deeply as any I have ever heard. "Almighty God, as we prepare [for] action from which some of us may not return, we humbly place our faith and trust in Thee. We do not pray for victory, nor even for our individual safety. But we pray for help that none of us may let a comrade down—that each of us may do his duty to himself, to his comrades and his country, and so be worthy of our American heritage." I walked away with tears in my eyes, dropping into the sand.

Eisenhower then "used the occasion to engage in his long-standing habit of seeking solitude," as he looked out at the moonlit desert in quiet contemplation.

On another occasion, in Algiers, Ike was scheduled to meet one morning with Churchill concerning the upcoming invasion of Sicily. Early that morning, a West Point classmate wandered down from the city toward the Mediterranean shoreline. There he saw Eisenhower in contemplation alone:

> As I approached a deserted section of the beach I saw Ike seated on the wreckage of a small boat, facing out to sea. In his hand was a crusty, ripped canteen cover which had been half buried among the other military debris discarded on the sand. I stopped and watched Ike. He stared at the canteen cover a long while, then looked out across the sea. Finally, he folded the cover carefully and placed it inside the boat, stood up, adjusted his cap firmly, and strode off to his staff car which was parked up the beach.

With a renewed "inner peace," Eisenhower then returned to his office for the meeting.

ONE SOURCE OF frustration for Eisenhower was the best combat leader under his command, namely George Patton. Patton had already created big trouble for Eisenhower and himself when, in incidents a week apart in August 1943, Patton slapped one shell-shocked soldier and then another at field hospitals in Sicily. Eisenhower agonized over what to do about the incidents; Butcher wrote in his diary that "Ike is deeply concerned and has scarcely slept for several nights, trying to figure out the wisest way of handling this dilemma." After reflecting on it, Eisenhower wrote a stern letter to Patton—for decades, his close friend—in which he described the incidents as "shocking" and said that "I must so seriously question your good judgment and your self-discipline as to raise serious doubt in my mind about your future usefulness." He added: "No letter that I have been called upon to write in my military career has caused me the mental anguish of this one." Through an intermediary, Eisenhower then directed Patton to apologize to the two men, which he did. (On Patton's own initiative, he also apologized in general terms to each of his units, in speeches laced with off-script profanity.) To Marshall, Eisenhower described Patton's superb generalship during the fighting in Sicily, but added, in reference to the slapping incidents, that "General Patton continues to exhibit some of those unfortunate personal traits of which you and I have always known." Ike concluded of Patton: "He has qualities that we cannot afford to lose unless he ruins himself."

Patton tested the "unless" clause of that sentence eight months later, when in a speech to a British social club he stated that, "since it seems to be the destiny of America and Great Britain to rule the world, the better we know each other the better off we will be." The press pounced on the statement. (Patton's offense was to leave the Soviets out of the ruling group.) The *Washington Post* editorialized, "General Patton has progressed from simple assaults on individuals to collective assault on entire nationalities." A now-forgotten congressman from North Dakota likewise charged that Patton had slapped "the face of every one of the United Nations, except Great Britain."

The episode came at the worst possible time for Eisenhower, since D-day was then only weeks away, and he was under enormous stress as a result. Eisenhower had a notorious temper, and on this occasion it snapped. To Omar Bradley—other than Eisenhower, the top American general in Europe—Ike said, "I'm just about fed up," and intimated that he would remove Patton from command. Bradley—dour, gray, humorless, a man who detested Patton from the start—wrote that "I fully concurred in Ike's decision to send Patton home. I, too, was fed up." To Marshall, Eisenhower wrote in an April 29 cable that "I have sent for Patton to allow him opportunity to present his case personally to me. On all of the evidence now available I will relieve him from command." In his place, Eisenhower proposed General Courtney Hodges, who Eisenhower said "can do a very fine job as Third Army commander. The big difference is that Patton has proved his ability to conduct a ruthless drive whereas Hodges has not." That was a big difference indeed. Ike then went on to discuss potential assignments for Patton after he was sent home.

Crucially, however, Eisenhower followed that cable with a letter to Patton himself—in which Ike gave full vent to his anger and frustration with his longtime friend. Eisenhower wrote that "I must tell you frankly that I regard this incident with the utmost seriousness and you should understand thoroughly that it is still filled with drastic potentialities regarding yourself." Ike went on: "I have warned you time and again against your impulsiveness in action and speech and have flatly instructed you to say nothing that could be misinterpreted by either your own subordinates or by the public." Then his criticism became even more personal:

> You first came into my command at my own insistence because I believed in your fighting qualities and your ability to lead troops in battle. At the same time I have always been fully aware of your habit of dramatizing yourself and committing indiscretions for no other apparent purpose than of calling attention to yourself. I am thoroughly weary of your failure to control your tongue and have begun to doubt your all-round judgment, so essential in high military position.

In that last sentence—that Ike had "begun to doubt" Patton's fitness for command—one sees irresolution begin to creep in. Above all, Eisenhower felt overwhelming pressure to make the Normandy invasion, Operation Overlord, a success. Just three days before, Marshall had reminded Eisenhower that "you carry the burden of responsibility as to the success of OVERLORD." And now Eisenhower had poured out his frustration to Patton in the most brutal and personal terms. The effect must have been cathartic; and at some level Eisenhower must have known that the persons who would be most happy to see Patton sent home would not be members of Congress or Bradley or the *Washington Post*, but the Germans themselves. They feared Patton as they did no other American general—as Ike well knew.

Marshall deftly guided the outcome from there. His response to Eisenhower's April 29 cable was one of the more consequential of the war. In an earlier cable, Marshall had transcended the emotion surrounding the affair, telling Ike that "like you I have been considering the matter on a purely business basis"—a veiled admonition, to be sure—and noting further that Patton was the only American general with actual experience fighting Rommel, who then commanded the German coastal defenses. Now that Eisenhower was proposing to remove Patton outright, Marshall responded with cool, measured indirection. In a cable dated May 2, Marshall wrote: "The decision is exclusively yours. My view, and it is merely that, is that you should not weaken your hand for OVERLORD . . . Do not consider War Department position in the matter. Consider only OVERLORD and your own heavy burden of responsibility for its success. Everything else is of minor importance."

Catharsis and cool reflection won out. Two days later Eisenhower cabled to Patton: "I am once more taking the responsibility of retaining you in command in spite of damaging repercussions from a personal indiscretion. I do this solely because of my faith in you as a battle leader and from no other motives." Later events in Europe—notably Patton's brilliant performance, in contrast to Hodges's lethargy, during the Allies' desperate struggle in the Battle of the Bulge—would fully vindicate Eisenhower's decision.

EISENHOWER'S PRACTICE OF thinking by writing intensified after his appointment as Supreme Commander of the Allied invasion of Europe. In another memo for his diary, written by hand and dated February 7, 1944, Eisenhower tersely began: "In early December the President told me I was to move to England to become the Supreme Commander, Allied Expeditionary Forces." He then surveyed the problems before him. As usual there was a shortage of landing craft, "a need that cannot be ignored." Relatedly, "the fighting in the Pacific is absorbing far too much of our limited resources during this *critical* phase of the European war . . . The forthcoming operation should have every resource the two nations can produce until the moment when the invading force is established on the continent." But the most serious problem lay with the invasion plan itself: "The fatal defect, in my opinion, was that all of the planning had been done on the basis of a 3-division assault," whereas Eisenhower was convinced that the invasion required five divisions. Eisenhower noted that the British and American Chiefs of Staff "were still considering the problem." But with his thoughts thus clarified, and with Montgomery's assistance, Eisenhower soon convinced them.

The seven days before D-day itself, however, best exemplified Eisenhower's use of productive solitude. By the third week of May 1944, after immense preparation, Eisenhower felt that "the only remaining great decision to be faced before D-day was that of fixing, definitely, the day and hour of the assault." That decision was itself highly complex: the invasion required a combination of clear skies for air operations, a full moon for the paratrooper drop behind enemy lines the night before, moderate seas for the ships, and tides low enough to allow the landing craft to run ashore before striking the obstacles, many of them mined, that the Germans had placed near the high-water mark. But on May 30 Eisenhower faced a fire in the rear. That day, the commander of the Allied Expeditionary Air Force, Sir Trafford Leigh-Mallory, came to Eisenhower's office to urge the cancellation of the paratroop drop and glider landings scheduled for the night before the invasion. Recent intelligence had indicated that one or more German divisions had reinforced the zones behind Utah Beach, in which the American paratroopers and glider troops would land. Leigh-Mallory now estimated that the paratroop divisions—the 82nd and 101st Airborne, some of the finest troops in the entire Army—would suffer 50 percent losses, and the glider troops 70 percent losses. A man known for his own physical courage, Leigh-Mallory pleaded with Eisenhower to avoid this "futile slaughter."

Eisenhower later wrote that "it would be difficult to conceive of a more soul-racking problem." Omar Bradley, the American general commanding the troops landing at Utah Beach, insisted that without the airborne drop the landing would fail. But if Leigh-Mallory was right, the Utah landing was hopeless anyway. Either outcome could lead to the failure of the invasion and "possibly Allied defeat in Europe." Eisenhower reacted as he often did in times of crisis:

> I went to my tent alone and sat down to think. I realized, of course, that if I disregarded the advice of my technical expert on the subject, and his predictions should prove accurate, then I would carry to my grave the unbearable burden of a conscience justly accusing me of the stupid, blind sacrifice of thousands of our flower of youth. Outweighing any personal burden, however, was the possibility that if he were right the effect of the disaster would be far more than local: it would be likely to spread to the entire force.

Turning the issue "over and over" in his mind, Eisenhower "finally narrowed the critical points" to these: if he canceled the airborne operation, he would have to cancel the Utah landing, which itself was essential to success on D-day; Leigh-Mallory's estimate was only that, an estimate; and the other airborne commanders—including General Matthew Ridgway, who was himself scheduled to parachute in with the 82nd Airborne the night before the invasion—had always supported the operation. Eventually, Eisenhower picked up the phone, called Leigh-Mallory, and told him the operation would proceed as planned.

But there remained the question of the weather. On the morning of June 3—after a frustrating meeting with Charles de Gaulle, who had refused to assist the invasion unless Roosevelt first recognized him as ruler of France—Eisenhower did what he frequently did after frustrating meetings, which was to retreat to his office and distill his thoughts into a memo. That morning Eisenhower must have had a sense of déjà vu: thirty months before, on the eve of another amphibious invasion—Operation Torch, the allied invasion of North Africa—and moreover after a frustrating meeting with a different French leader, the incompetent Henri Giraud,

Eisenhower had sat down at his desk at Gibraltar and typed out his ten-point memo, "Worries of a Commander." On this morning, June 3, 1944, Eisenhower went to his tent once more and prepared another list of worries, several of which concerned de Gaulle. Eisenhower also worried about the Germans' shoreline defenses, and about whether Allied bombing had succeeded in destroying the routes by which the Germans would seek to reinforce their forces around the landing sites. But Eisenhower's greatest worry was the weather, a factor that could serve as a force multiplier for either the Allies or Germans the morning of the invasion, depending on which way it broke. For miles around Eisenhower's tent, and indeed all around the coast of England, the invasion force sat tense, as Eisenhower put it, like "a great human spring, coiled for the moment when its energy should be released and it would vault the English Channel in the greatest amphibious assault ever attempted." And on Eisenhower's shoulders alone would rest the decision whether to uncoil the mighty spring two mornings hence.

Stephen Ambrose writes that "one of Eisenhower's characteristics was his desire to simplify. Faced with a complex situation, he usually tried to separate it into its essentials, extract a principal point, and then make that point his guiding star for all decisions." This morning Eisenhower did precisely that, sifting out the factors on each side until he wrote out a single rule to guide him: "We must go unless there is a real and very serious deterioration in the weather."

But the very next morning, a "very serious deterioration" is exactly what Eisenhower ran into. Each day that first week of June, at four A.M. and again at nine thirty P.M., in the library of a nearby Georgian mansion called Southwick House, Eisenhower and his top lieutenants met with their top meteorologist, Captain J. M. Stagg. A Scotsman with an air of dignified reserve, Stagg was an unsung hero of D-day, "a scientist to his bones with all of the scientist's refined capacity to pass unimpassioned judgment on the evidence, a man of sharp mind and soft speech, detached, resolute, courageous." Earlier Stagg had predicted fair weather for June 5, the scheduled date for the invasion. But at the meeting the morning of June 4, Stagg reported an unwelcome change: a meteorological vessel seven hundred miles west of Ireland had reported a powerful incoming storm, bringing with it the lowest barometric pressures ever recorded that century around the British Isles in June. Eisenhower's test was met; he pushed back the invasion to June 6.

But seventeen hours later, at the nine thirty P.M. meeting on June 4, Stagg reported another change: although the wind and rain still rattled the windowpanes of the room as he spoke, Stagg said the storm would relent soon, followed by decent weather the night of June 5 and throughout the day on June 6—but perhaps followed again by stormy weather on June 7. Eisenhower thus faced a dilemma: if he proceeded on June 6, he might get the first waves of troops ashore but then be prevented by bad weather from reinforcing them the following day. If Eisenhower now delayed the invasion even a single day, however, the moon and tides would not permit another attempt until June 19, an almost unbearable prospect with hundreds of thousands of men on the knife's edge of readiness all around him. Eisenhower walked over to a window and looked out at the driving, nearly horizontal rain. For a long while he said nothing. Watching him, his chief of staff was struck by "the loneliness and isolation of a commander at a time when such a momentous decision was to be taken by him, with full knowledge that success or failure rests on his individual decision."

Yet Eisenhower had already identified the key variable for his decision. In his memo reciting his list of worries the morning before, Eisenhower had written that "we must go unless there is a real and very serious deterioration in the weather." Now, as he looked out at the driving rain on the night of June 4, the prospect of bad weather for June 7 was still only that: a prospect. Finally, still looking out the window, Eisenhower calmly said, "I am quite positive that the order must be given."

At the four A.M. meeting the following morning, June 5—with the invasion fleet already steaming into the Channel, but still not too late to turn them back—Eisenhower considered the question a final time. Stagg reported that his forecast had not changed, but cautioned that it had not gotten any better either. Eisenhower canvassed the group a final time, pacing with hands clasped behind his back as he did so. Then he sank into a sofa, where for an agonizing five minutes he silently pondered his decision. Finally he broke into a broad smile and said, "Well Stagg, if this forecast comes off, I promise you we'll have a celebration when the time comes." Then he gave the order, which was now final: "Okay, let's go."

Within a minute the room emptied, leaving Eisenhower alone. Again he went to his tent, where he sat down and wrote out a press release to be used in case of failure: "Our landings in the Cherbourg-Havre area have failed to gain a satisfactory foothold and I have withdrawn the troops. My decision to attack at this time and place was based on the best information available. The troops, the air and the Navy did all that Bravery and devotion to duty could do. If any blame or fault attaches to the attempt it is mine alone."

That evening Eisenhower drove up to visit the 101st Airborne— the men Leigh-Mallory had pleaded with him not to send—as they blacked their faces and packed their gear for the flight to Normandy, now only hours away. Walking among the men, he offered whatever advice he could: "The idea, the perfect idea, is to keep moving." Finally he stood by the runway, watching the twin-engined C-47s take off one by one into the night, filled with those "thousands of our flower of youth"—all of them headed into the fire of Normandy. Just after midnight, as the last plane roared away, Eisenhower's shoulders sagged. Then, his eyes full with tears, he turned to his driver and said: "Well, it's on."

CHAPTER 3

The Stillness of Intuition
Jane Goodall, 1960

"The first step on the road to experiencing true awareness is the cessation of noise from within."

—JANE GOODALL, *Reason for Hope*

Intuition and analytical clarity both involve processing information, but with intuition the processing is already done for you. The challenge with intuition is to access it. Usually our minds are caught up in a cycle of stimulus and response, sometimes about things worth thinking about, other times about trivialities. This cycle creates a mental dialogue of its own, which during times of constant inputs or stress is more like a din. So long as the dialogue continues, our attention is consumed by it.

Intuition, by contrast, forms beneath the surface of conscious thought. Intuition (or instinct, as it is sometimes called) is not focused solely on what one is experiencing now, but instead draws upon all of one's experiences, past and present. Intuition makes connections between all those experiences. Frequently those connections are based on patterns: when one has perceived certain things in the past, certain other things were also present, or soon followed. That a person glances to the side as he speaks, for example, might give rise to an intuition that he is lying—for one has encountered that sort of side-glance before. That a longtime city-dweller perceives another person following her on a city street, at a certain distance and with a certain gait, might give rise to an intuition of danger. And that a senior executive's office walls are covered with photographs of himself and various celebrities might give rise, to a middle manager meeting him for the first time, to an intuition that the executive is susceptible to flattery.

The mechanics of intuition and analytical thinking are opposites of one another. Analysis requires focus, which is to say that one's attention is concentrated on a single point. But intuition works best from a panoramic view, where one takes in all the surrounding circumstances—including details, like office décor, that at first might seem irrelevant. For those details give rise to patterns, which, when processed by the subconscious mind, give rise to intuition.

Intuition's critics are mistaken, therefore, to say that it is unreasoned. Reasoning based on patterns is a form of inductive reasoning (i.e., reasoning "from many specific observations to a general principle"; for example, that senior executives who cover their office walls with photos of themselves are generally narcissists), which in the case of intuition takes place subconsciously. (Analytical thinking is more commonly deductive, i.e., reasoning "from a general principle to a specific conclusion.") And because intuition is based on more information—in many cases vastly more—than analysis is, intuition provides an important check on analytical thinking. A particular analysis might be entirely coherent and yet entirely wrong—because it assumes a nonexistent fact or overlooks an existing one. Intuition will often catch the mistake. Of course, subconscious inductive reasoning based on circumstances one has encountered earlier in life has its limits, and thus so does intuition. But when analysis conflicts with intuition, intuition is usually right.

Unlike analytical thinking, however, intuition does its work silently—and thus often goes unnoticed. A person excited to see an old friend might not perceive, in his excitement, the import of his friend's eyes glancing away. A person looking back and forth at her phone might not perceive the danger from the person walking behind, even though she sees him. And the middle manager intimidated by a senior executive might not remember that he has seen office walls like that before. For intuition requires one not only to see, but to hear—to hear, specifically, a more quiet inner voice. True, sometimes intuition is emphatic; but more often it is subtle, modest, understated. And thus intuition usually requires mental quietude to break through the surface of conscious thought. Intuition therefore requires a deeper form of solitude: an absence of inputs not only from other minds, but also from one's own. It requires one not to process or agitate—but simply to perceive.

Intuition is thus not only a check upon analytical thought, but a complement to it. When analysis leads nowhere, intuition can often provide an answer. And when, as discussed above, analytical clarity leads to the identification of the critical variable upon which all depends, intuition can guide one's judgment about which way that variable will break. Given the space and quietude to operate, even if only for an instant—which for intuition is oftentimes enough—intuition can provide clarity when analytical thinking cannot.

Jane Goodall used intuition to magnificent effect in 1960, when studying chimpanzees in the mountains of central Africa. There she intuited that, if chimpanzees flee as if approached by a predator, that might be because, in seeking to approach them by stealth, one acts like a predator. And as her solitude grew more profound, Goodall perceived not only the connection between stealth and flight, but a more spiritual connection—between herself and all that existed around her.

SOMETIMES SOLITUDE IS part of what helps a person become a leader in the first place. In 1960, few people would have predicted that Jane Goodall would change the way that humans view their cohorts in the animal kingdom. Goodall was then twenty-six years old, with no undergraduate degree, no scientific training, and little scientific experience. She had come to Africa three years earlier, at the invitation of a friend from boarding school, and soon began working in Nairobi, Kenya, as a typist. But the following month she met Dr. Louis Leakey, the renowned archaeologist, who promptly hired her as his secretary. In that role she accompanied Leakey on expeditions throughout Kenya, digging up fossils in Olduvai Gorge and camping on the Serengeti.

Her timing was propitious. Although Leakey's fossils had yielded important clues about the diet, gait, and locomotion of mankind's earliest ancestors, their social interactions remained a mystery; as Goodall later wrote, "Behavior does not fossilize." But Leakey saw another way to explore those early relationships. Better than anyone, Leakey understood that modern humans shared a common ancestry with modern apes; and he reasoned that, if these modern primates shared certain behaviors, then their common ancestors likely shared those behaviors as well. Thus, to learn about the interactions of man's ancestors several million years before, Leakey proposed to study the interactions of modern apes today—particularly those of mankind's closest relative, the chimpanzees. Jane Goodall was the person whom Leakey chose to study them.

The project presented massive difficulties. Wild chimpanzees live only in remote African forests, where many other dangerous animals live as well. Chimps themselves are four times stronger than humans and can inflict a damaging bite. And like most wild animals, chimps are usually gone before an approaching human even knows they were there. Moreover, scientists at that time had little idea how to study chimpanzees; every prior attempt to do so had failed.

Leakey's plan was to send Goodall, alone with several African camp staff, to the Gombe Stream Chimpanzee Reserve, in what is now Tanzania. Gombe lies along the eastern shoreline of Lake Tanganyika, one of the largest, deepest (only Lake Superior is deeper), and cleanest lakes in the world, much longer than it is wide, running from north to south. Gombe itself comprises about thirty square miles of pristine tropical forest, in mountainous terrain, with streams tumbling downward toward the lake. In addition to chimpanzees, in 1960 the forest was home to baboons, monkeys, buffalo, a few leopards, many pythons, a wide variety of poisonous snakes (including three species of cobras), giant scorpions, and a few hippos and crocodiles along the shoreline.

Before Goodall arrived at Gombe, however, officials from the local game department imposed some changes to Leakey's plan. The officials refused to allow a European woman to travel to Gombe without another European to accompany her, so Goodall was joined by her mother, Vanne, who was always a source of strength for her. Another change, imposed at the last minute, was depressing: although Jane had planned to search for the chimpanzees alone, the officials now insisted that she be escorted by two "game scouts," ostensibly to ensure that she did not record seeing ten or twenty chimpanzees when she had seen only one.

Goodall arrived on the shores of Gombe in July 1960. Her early efforts portended failure: although during her first ten days she was able to see glimpses of chimps from a distance, through the heavy vegetation she could see nothing of their behavior. The next eight weeks were worse. Goodall saw even fewer chimps, usually from hundreds of yards away, and when she and her escorts did get closer to the chimps, they instantly fled. Goodall's intuition was to approach the chimps openly, rather than by stealth, as a predator would and as her unsuccessful predecessors had; but she also sensed that the chimps were more afraid of three observers than they would be of only one. Then, in August, Jane and Vanne came down with malaria, spiking temperatures as high as 105 degrees.

Jane's fever passed near the end of that month, though she was still weak. Early one morning she hiked up a nearby mountain alone, partly because she "could not bear the thought" of her escorts seeing her in such a weakened condition, but more, perhaps, to test her own intuition. She reached an ideal observation site— which she referred to thereafter as the Peak—and sat there, on a rock in plain view. Within fifteen minutes, she saw three chimpanzees on the bare slope directly below her, only eighty yards away. The chimps stared at Jane and then calmly moved away into some undergrowth. Soon a larger group of chimps descended the slope across from her, screaming and calling to each other before climbing some fig trees along the streambank in the valley below. Then, on the same bare slope below, another group of chimps appeared. They too stared at Jane and pattered down to the same line of fig trees. There the second group joined the first, wildly calling and violently swaying branches before settling down to feed. Eventually the chimps moved off as a single group, "following each other in a long, orderly line," with two infants "perched like jockeys on their mothers' backs." By following her own intuition—by positioning herself in plain view of the chimps, and by doing so alone—Goodall had made her first meaningful observation of their behavior.

That day, Goodall later wrote, "marked the turning point" in her study. Thereafter her escorts—who had always had trouble keeping up with her, and who by that point were pretty much worn out—were content to let her hike up to the Peak alone. There, each day, she was free to listen to and follow her own intuition—always wearing the same dull-colored clothes, never trying to follow or harass the chimps in any way, and thus not behaving as their predators might—until "the shy chimpanzees began to realize, at long last, that I was not so horrific and terrifying." Now she observed the chimps almost every day: passing by her in groups and singly and in pairs; some groups joining together, others breaking apart; members of one group calling out to members of another, who then responded from a distance; males charging at other males, sometimes dragging a branch or slapping the earth as they did so; quiet groups of females eating figs with their children; adult males embracing each other in greeting; juvenile chimps chasing each other through the treetops; and then, most importantly, an adult male using a thick stalk of grass as a tool to extract and then eat termites from an earthen mound.

Soon Jane began to recognize individual chimps. "As soon as I was sure of knowing a chimpanzee if I saw it again," she wrote, "I named it." Eventually Jane came to know scores of chimps, and to see precisely the variations in temperament, motivation, and behavior that, among humans, we call personality. There was Mr. McGregor, an older male with only a tonsure of hair circling his scalp, who would raise his head indignantly when startled, and who reminded Jane, "for some reason, of Beatrix Potter's old gardener in *The Tale of Peter Rabbit*." There was Flo, an older female with thinning hair, teeth worn down to the gums, ragged ears, and a "deformed, bulbous nose," who "had a relaxed and friendly relationship with most of the adult males." For some reason the males were wildly attracted to her sexually; when Flo was fertile, "it was impossible for her to sit up or lie down without several pairs of eyes instantly swiveling in her direction, and if she got up to move on, the males were on their feet in no time." And Flo "was a highly competent mother, affectionate, tolerant, playful, and protective," who would spend hours tickling, chasing, and turning somersaults with her young children. Once, with Flo sitting nearby, Flo's young son Flint was teasing Crease, an adult male chimp, shaking a rain-soaked branch above Crease's head and showering him with drops. Eventually Crease lost his temper and leapt up, threatening Flint. "At once Flo sprang into action. Sticking her few remaining moth-eaten hairs on end she charged at Crease, uttering fierce waa-barks of threat." But in contrast there was Passion, a loner, who was "a cold mother, intolerant and brusque, and she seldom played with her infant, particularly during the first two years." More darkly, Passion was a psychopath among chimpanzees: a cannibal (a rarity among chimps, as among humans) who stalked mothers of newborn chimps and—after beating the screaming mother into submission—would snatch the infant away, clutch it to her own breast, and then go off somewhere and eat it.

But there was also the gentle David Greybeard, a handsome adult male, "calm and unafraid," the first chimp who allowed Jane to approach up close, who drew termites from the mound with his blade of grass, and who on one occasion was following Jane when she thought she was following him. Perhaps Jane's most profound interaction with any chimpanzee came on a day when she was following David through a lush tropical valley. At one point they were sitting next to each other. Jane saw a ripe palm nut, and dared to hold it out for him. She described what happened next:

He gave my offering a scornful glance and turned away. I held
my hand a little nearer. For a few more moments he continued to
ignore me. And then, suddenly, he turned towards me, reached
out his hand to the nut, and, to my astonishment and delight,
held my hand with his, keeping a firm warm pressure for about
10 seconds. He then withdrew his hand, glanced at the nut, and
dropped it to the ground.

David had taken her hand to reassure her, Jane explained, and
"then demonstrated his complete lack of interest in my offering by
dropping it to the ground."

In these encounters, what Goodall described as her naïveté—or,
one might say, her isolation from other professionals in her field—
was an asset for her. In 1960 it was not permissible in scientific
circles to regard the members of any species, other than humans,
as individuals. One spoke of the behavior of "chimpanzees" generally, but a proper scientist would not have attributed distinct
personalities to them. And Jane "had no idea," she wrote, "that it
would have been more appropriate to assign each of the chimpanzees a number rather than a name when I got to know him or her."
Jane was as uncorrupted by the standards of professionals in her
field, as they were by actual knowledge of chimpanzees; and as a
result she drew closer to the chimps.

BY JANUARY 1961, Vanne had returned to England and Jane's
escorts had left her. Jane genuinely missed her mother after she
left; but what came next, Goodall later wrote, was "a period I
remember vividly, not only because I was beginning to accomplish
something at last, but also because of the delight I felt in being
completely by myself." In the months of "solitude" that followed—
in her spiritual memoir, *Reason for Hope*, she devotes a chapter of
that name to this period—Goodall moved beyond her intuitions
about how best to observe the chimps, to a more profound understanding of their place in the forest, and of her own.

"The first step on the road to experiencing true awareness," she
wrote, "is the cessation of noise from within." In the stillness of

intuition, and with "aloneness" now "a way of life," Jane found herself "getting closer to animals and nature, and as a result, getting closer to myself and more and more in tune with the spiritual power I felt all around." She perceived with new clarity the forest world around her. "The feel of rough sun-warmed bark of an ancient forest giant, or the cool, smooth skin of a young and eager sapling, gave me a strange, intuitive sense of the sap as it was sucked up by unseen roots and drawn up to the very tips of the branches." Her perceptions became even clearer when she focused simply on perceiving them. "Words are part of our rational selves, and to abandon them for a while is to give freer rein to our intuitive selves." Thus, she wrote, "it is all but impossible to describe the new awareness that comes when words are abandoned."

That awareness for Goodall was often spiritual. "No words of mine could ever convey, even in part, the almost mystical awareness of beauty and eternity that accompanies certain treasured moments." In *Through a Window*, she describes one such moment after a rainstorm in the forest:

> The air was filled with a feathered symphony, the evensong of birds. I heard new frequencies in their music and, too, in the singing of insect voices, notes so high and sweet that I was amazed. I was intensely aware of the shape, the colour, of individual leaves, the varied patterns of the veins that made each one unique. Scents were clear, easily identifiable—fermenting, over-ripe fruit; water-logged earth; cold, wet bark; the damp odour of chimpanzee hair, and, yes, my own too. And the aromatic scent of young, crushed leaves was almost overpowering. I sensed the presence of a bushbuck, then saw him, quietly browsing upwind, his spiraled horns dark with rain. And I was utterly filled with that peace "which passeth all understanding."

In moments like these—moments she could experience only in absolute solitude—Goodall came to realize that, even as a human being, she was not set apart from nature, but entirely a part of it, just as the chimps were. The experience was deeply spiritual, as she

perceived a grand unity with everything around her, and everything that came before. Reflecting upon these experiences
afterward, Goodall realized that her empathy with the chimpanzees, borne of this unity, had guided her intuition as she observed
them.

That same empathy, and the sense of unity that gave rise to it,
became the foundation for Goodall's effectiveness as a leader. With
that foundation, in later years, she was able to persuade millions of
people, all over the world, to embrace her understanding of chimpanzees—and indeed all animals—as mankind's companions,
rather than subjects, in the animal kingdom.

PART II

CHAPTER 4

Creativity

Although Marie Curie conducted much of her research jointly with her husband, Pierre, one of her most far-reaching discoveries came while working alone. In March 1897, in Paris, she began research for a doctorate in science, something no woman in Europe had obtained before. The year before, another scientist working in France, Henri Becquerel, had wrapped several photographic plates in black cloth and covered them with a sheet of aluminum, on top of which he placed some crystals containing uranium. Then he placed the whole package in a drawer and closed the door. Removing the plates several days later, he was astounded to find that they were intensely fogged where the crystals had lain above them. Becquerel's discovery was that uranium salts emit rays that—like X-rays, which had been discovered in late 1895—penetrate matter. Now Marie Curie sought to answer a question raised by Becquerel's discovery: from where did the uranium compound get the energy that darkened the plates? Working in a small room with borrowed instruments and scavenged mineral samples, Curie put different substances on a metal plate and then measured the energy—in the form of electric current—that passed between the substance on the plate and another metal plate placed nearby. She discovered that the energy emitted by the uranium compounds depended solely upon the amount of uranium in the compound; the other elements in the compound (unless the elements were themselves radioactive), or whether the compound was wet or dry, made no difference to the amount of energy emitted. And Curie's compounds appeared completely unchanged as they emitted their electrical current. The results seemed to violate the first law of thermodynamics: that energy can be converted from one form to another—as with an ordinary chemical reaction that gives off heat or light—but cannot be created or destroyed. What Curie had discovered was that the energy emitted by uranium came not from any chemical reaction but from the uranium atom itself. This new form of energy Marie Curie called "radiation." From that discovery, later scientists deduced the structure of the atom—and the previously unimaginable forces that lay within it.

IF CLARITY SERVES to identify which of the available options will be most effective for a leader, creativity serves to develop a possibility the leader was not aware of before. Sometimes, as Mihaly Csikszentmihalyi describes in his seminal book *Creativity*, a creative work or idea is one based on rejection of established norms in the relevant field. Beethoven's *Eroica* symphony—which exploded the rigid symphonic form used until then—is an example. So was Ulysses S. Grant's decision to cut his own supply lines at Vicksburg. On other occasions a work is creative not because it rejects what came before, but simply because its content is new. Marie Curie's discovery of radiation is an example. And on still other occasions an idea is creative because it is based on horizontal connections between things that at first seem unrelated.

AS WITH CLARITY, there is an intuitive path to creativity, on which much of the work is already done for the leader, if only he will pause to listen. Joey Reiman makes a point of spending time on that path, finding connections between his clients' products and ways to assuage society's ills. "The best creative idea I've ever had was to create a company whose foundation is thoughtfulness," says Reiman, founder and CEO of BrightHouse, a consulting firm in Atlanta. Joey himself combines intuitive creativity with a joyful, almost effervescent embrace of spiritual values. In 1975, when Joey was twenty-two, he was a passenger during a near-fatal car crash in Rome. "My right arm and hand were paralyzed," he says. "The doctor told me I'd never use them again. I was in the hospital for three months. At the time, that felt like loneliness rather than solitude." From his hospital bed, Joey recalls, "I made a pact with God: if I got my hand back, I would do something purposeful in my life."

Joey did recover full use of his hand, but the pact drifted away from his mind. He entered the advertising business and eventually founded his own firm, which was highly successful. Yet he was unhappy with his work. "I was troubled by the metrics of the advertising business," he says. "We were convincing people to buy things they don't need, and creating needs they don't want." In 1994, his firm became part of a larger advertising firm. Joey attended a firm-wide meeting in London the following year. "One of the firm's executives gave a speech about how to 'keep your clients fresh.' I realized the work I was doing then, the money, the prestige, it was all meaningless. That was a spear-in-the-chest moment for me."

Joey left the meeting and spent the afternoon walking along the Thames River. "I thought to myself, 'I'm not going to spend the rest of my life refrigerating clients. I'm not in the refrigeration business.'" Another leader profiled later in this chapter, Chip Edens, observes that "the grand invitation is to embrace the reality of your life and to figure out what to do with it." Joey accepted that invitation during his walk along the Thames. "I had a revelation then," he says. "A revelation is the collision of information, intuition, and your highest values. My revelation was that my time in the hospital had not been loneliness. It was actually solitude, because it was productive. Twenty years later, I suddenly understood that I needed to do something purposeful with my life." He asked himself, "What if I could build a company based on thoughtfulness?" Joey's idea was to reject the norms of the business he had been working in until then. Rather than feed consumer appetites, he thought, "I could create a company whose messages would heal, inspire, guide the world to a better place."

Joey's company is BrightHouse, which he describes as "the world's first ideation company." "Ideation is the process of thinking," he says. "Our clients pay us for our thinking time. We need to spend time daydreaming, free-thinking to generate ideas. It's not wasting time. Einstein once described his typical day at Princeton as teaching class twenty percent of the time, and eighty percent of the time staring out the window."

Joey describes the mission of BrightHouse. "Our focus is to bring light to the companies that work with us, and make them a source of light in the world. First we do our due diligence. We learn about the company, its history, its identity. And then we generalize that into a new ethos, and think about some larger purpose that is consistent with its history and identity. How can this company mitigate society's ills?"

Joey describes how BrightHouse fosters creativity. "Our work cycle for a project is four to sixteen weeks. It's a model of deep incubation. Solitude is absolutely essential to that process." He emphasizes the importance of thinking in what he calls "environments of unconditioned response." "Those are where the best ideas come. It's an environment that doesn't direct a response. There are no protocols." The opposite, he says, "is a 'cubi-kill.' A cubicle puts you inside a literal box. You're thinking within the rules there. Codification, routinization, stratification, all of those things are the enemies of unconditioned response." Those kinds of regulated environments confine one's thinking to channels dug out in advance. Environments of unconditioned response, in contrast, allow one's thoughts to find their own streambed.

Joey describes what he calls the "last bastions" of unconditioned response. "The first is a church," he says. The effect is similar to what other people feel in the mountains. "I was born Jewish, I go to temple, but the architecture of a church, the spires, they literally inspire. The surroundings bring you to the intersection of earth and heaven." Another is the car. "It's crazy to play music in the car. It's one of the only times you can think." Another is the shower, a place where a person is usually protected from outside inputs. "It's warm, private, there's water, white noise, there's nothing to direct your thinking a certain way." A remaining bastion is "the park. You're among the flora, the fauna, the air. You're not just connecting with it. You're communing with it, a part of it." In places like these, Joey says, "you can hear thoughts that are only whispered to you. You can divine, which means to discover by intuition or insight. You go inside for the sight."

One example of BrightHouse's work was done for Pepperidge Farm, the manufacturer of Goldfish crackers. "Margaret Rudkin was the company's founder," Joey says. "In researching the product we learned that her son had near-fatal allergies, which were aggravated by preservatives and artificial ingredients. She began to make all-natural bread for her son, and then founded the company to sell it in New York. So part of the company's DNA was to help kids be healthy. Meanwhile, when we were working on the project, in 2004, childhood depression was at unprecedented levels. We connected those two things and thought about ways our client could help that problem. We came up with the idea of 'fishfulthinking.com.' Today it's the number-one website for children's and parents' cognitive health." Joey credits BrightHouse's "longer, incubation pace" for the idea. "If we had moved at a faster, business pace, we never would have excavated that original brand identity and then generalized it into a new ethos.

"There is nothing more important in a leader's arsenal than solitude," Joey concludes. "That's where we find revelation."

As with clarity, there is an analytical path to creativity. That path is hacked out by hard work, as the leader sorts and synthesizes the available data, this time to work out a novel solution.

Dena Braeger follows that approach as the mother of six young children in El Paso, Texas. "Parenting is the oldest form of leadership," she says. "We have a cultural norm that leadership takes place outside the home, not inside. My leadership is as important as being a CEO." Dena has broad experience with leadership, having graduated from West Point and served as a company commander in Iraq in 2003. She later earned a master's degree in psychology from Columbia University. "As a company commander, the expectation was that you were constantly accessible," she says. "I had to tell my people, 'I'm going to be by myself for an hour.' I needed solitude to be more committed to my leadership during the other times." The same is true for her as a parent. "The other day I got a babysitter for an hour. I went hiking by myself. I think more deeply then, and think about things I didn't plan to think about."

Dena talks about the problem of information overload. "The place hardest hit is the household. Everyone is constantly online or on their phone. I have a lot of 'no-electronic' time for the kids. Figure out what you want to do. Create it rather than have it handed to you." She sees the same problem with adults. "People make such an effort to copy what other people do, because we have so much access to information." She cites an example. "I'm surrounded by people on Pinterest. I'll be damned if I make something on Pinterest," she says. "You'll see things like these cupcakes that look amazing. And people copy them. But on the inside they're phony, because the person didn't create it themselves. We're getting more of everything, but less of what is authentically ourselves. If we spent more time alone, creating something that might not look as amazing but is more authentic, we'd value ourselves more."

Dena uses reflection to develop creative solutions to problems she encounters as a parent. "The other day my daughter was mean to her sister, being dramatic, taking offense at everything," Dena says. "I was super-irritated, and I disciplined her in the moment. But I decided to craft a more thoughtful response in solitude. I need to be able to think for more than a few seconds about the complexities of being a parent." For two days, Dena reflected on the incident. "I realized that what was really irritating me was her quickness to take offense," Dena says. "It's not just a surface problem. As a leader, you always have the power to discipline people. But I didn't want to crush her. I wanted to approach the problem with empathy, rather than just discipline. I wanted to inspire her." Eventually Dena worked out a response. "I decided to lay out for her the things she's doing well, and point out where's she's stumbling. I thought about a way I can coach her about those things. I decided to talk about what offenses mean, and explain that people will disappoint you at times you expect and don't expect, and that a more peaceful way to go through life is not to be constantly offended by these things."

Dena draws some larger lessons from the experience. "Often we try to correct behavior without going to the heart of it," she says. "That takes time. If you don't take the time, you just deal with the problem in the moment.

"As a parent and a leader," Dena concludes, "there's a complexity to interpersonal relationships. You need to take the time to find creative solutions to the problems you encounter."

TIM HALL IS the head coach of the cycling team at Lees-McRae College in North Carolina, which in cycling circles is known as "the Alabama of college cycling." He reflected on his life experiences to create a team culture out of whole cloth. "I was actually a baseball player when I was younger," he says. "I attended Cumberland College, about thirty miles outside Nashville, and was drafted by the Padres. I played four years for the Padres and Braves in the minor leagues. They pretty much tell you when it's over." When he was done with baseball, Tim went back to school, got an M.B.A., and then sold building supplies for a wholesaler. In 2001, as the building industry slowed down, Tim was laid off. For eighteen months, he was unable to find a job. Then, in October 2002, while making a left turn on his bicycle in downtown Nashville, Tim was struck by a Jeep Cherokee. "My left tibia was snapped in half," he says. "All I could think of was, 'I've been a burden on my family, and now I've just doubled the burden. They'll have to take care of me.'"

Looking back, Tim describes the accident as "a pivotal moment" for him. "I'm glad I got hit by that car," he says. "I was laid up in my sister's old bed, literally with the repo man knocking at the door. It made me think about how I got in that position, that moment right there. I realized I needed to make different decisions going forward."

After his leg had healed, Tim applied for a job in a family-owned restaurant chain that paid eight dollars per hour. "I wasn't above doing any kind of work. I was nervous walking in to fill out the application. Two weeks later, they offered me the job, with no promises for advancement." Yet after six months, Tim was promoted to assistant manager at one of the company's restaurants. Two years later he was the general manager of a $3 million restaurant, supervising twenty-five employees. "That's where my leadership skills got challenged," he says. "I had to run the organization, plus hire, train, and fire, if necessary, a group of employees with very diverse skills and abilities."

In 2004, Tim's alma mater, Cumberland College, started a cycling team. A year later, the team's head coach left the program. "I was making pretty good money at the time, but I was intrigued by the position. My heart was in sports, and I'd gained leadership skills in the restaurant business." Tim's former baseball coach arranged an interview, and soon Tim was offered the position. He accepted it, even though his pay would be cut in half. "I'll never forget telling my boss at the restaurant about it. He just looked at me and said, 'Man, I'm so jealous. I'd do anything to follow something I'm passionate about. I support you a hundred percent.'"

Soon Tim found himself coaching a sport that he had not played himself while in college (he began competitive cycling in 2000) and that was just getting started nationwide. "It was a creativity challenge," he says. "I had to create my own system. There was no template for a collegiate cycling team. I realized I needed to reflect on how I was going to do this."

Tim started an early-morning reflection practice that he continues to this day. "I make a cup of coffee, sit, and think, looking out at the bird feeder. No electronic devices." ("I never thought of it as solitude before," he says. "I thought of it as my quiet time.") Each morning, Tim reflected back on his experiences as a player and in the restaurant business. "I realized that my leadership had to start with myself. Once, when I was in the food business, a brilliant young employee said to me, 'You're dogmatic.' I had thought I was open-minded. But the way she said it pushed me back. I thought there must be some truth to it. So as a coach, I try not to be dogmatic." He also thought back to lessons he had learned from his baseball coach at Cumberland. "His big thing was, always act as if you've got eyes on you. On and off the field. Be a beacon of responsibility." Another lesson from his playing days was that "you remember the *relationships*—with your teammates, the coaches—not the victories. Create the right relationships, and you'll win." And Tim recalled his central leadership lesson as a manager in the restaurant business. "You have to state what your expectations are in advance. You can't make up expectations as you go along. It's not fair."

During mornings in front of the bird feeder, Tim eventually distilled his reflections down to a statement of "Team Expectations," which he calls "the Three Cs—Character, Classroom, and Competitor." "It's a statement of principles, not rules. It's an aspirational tool, not a corrective tool. It's meant to create a culture. You need to share your vision as a leader, and get your people engaged in it." The order of Tim's Cs reflects his priorities as a leader. "Character" includes things like "treat everyone with respect," "set good examples for others," and "do what you say you will do." "Classroom" includes "attend all classes" and "communicate with your instructors and earn their respect." "Competitor" is about professionalism, with admonitions like "be humble and gracious in victory or defeat," "accept constructive criticism in order to improve," and "be selfless toward your teammates and cycling program." Tim recalls when he presented his Team Expectations for the first time. "I could tell that the athletes embraced it. They didn't think it was BS. It gets my athletes to reflect on why they came here, what our purpose is."

Now, as cycling coach at Lees-McRae, Tim uses his mornings a different way. "I have more time to go on offense, rather than just problem-solve." But his ultimate goal remains the same. "When I meet each one of my athletes' parents, I want to be able to look them in the eye knowing that I took great care of their kid."

MONTGOMERY MEIGS'S APPROACH to creativity is modeled on the hard analytical style of Ulysses S. Grant. "The concentration afforded by time alone enables a leader to find unique solutions to tough problems," says Meigs, formerly commander of the United States Army in Europe. Meigs now serves as a senior lecturer at the University of Texas. In 1998, he was commander of the NATO Stabilization Force in Bosnia, after the three-year civil war there. Among his responsibilities, he recalls, was "to inculcate in the military leaders of the Croat, Bosniak, and Bosnian Serb forces the values needed in a democratic military." The challenge was daunting: the leadership of all three factions was rife with corruption, and none of them had meaningful experience with civilian control of the military. Meigs got little help from his superiors. "I suggested to my NATO boss that we create training programs for these forces in NATO military schools, but he made clear he had no funds for the effort. I was on my own," he says. "There was also a lot of pressure from Washington and the other NATO capitals for quick results."

Meigs's response was to follow an example from history. A few years before, while preparing for a talk on leadership, Meigs had researched Grant's Vicksburg campaign. After repeated failures to take the Confederate fortress there, Grant holed up for several days in an office on board a river steamship. He emerged with the most radical military plan of the entire war. "If Grant could come up with such an innovative solution to problems far greater than mine, his example was useful," Meigs says. "I didn't have a river steamer to go to. But alone in my office and in my sleeping quarters, I pondered the problem. How could we influence the values of these military cadres without funds or institutional help from NATO?"

Like Grant more than a century before, Meigs pulled together the information available to him and analyzed his way to a solution. He found the beginnings of one in an obscure provision of the Dayton Peace Treaty. "Under Annex 1A of the treaty, I could veto any promotion to flag rank in any of the military factions. I could also veto the assignment of any of their generals to new positions within their military," Meigs says. "So the first thing we did was that nobody was promoted to flag rank or reassigned without my approval." The factions soon put Meigs to the test. "The first case involved an unsavory officer who had a very questionable record during the war and whose professional experience prior to joining the paramilitary forces had been as a dancing instructor." Meigs rejected the man's assignment to an important military position.

The second part of Meigs's solution was likewise based on his powers as commander of the NATO Stabilization Force. "We formed an Office of the Inspector General to investigate misconduct by their generals," Meigs says. "We put a U.S. colonel with experience as an inspector general in charge of the office. We also assigned two officers from each faction in the office. That way, in any investigation, one officer from the subject's own military and another from a different faction would conduct the investigation. That combination ensured the impartiality of the results." One of the office's first investigations involved the commanding general of one of the factions. "He was using soldiers to build his new house," Meigs says. "We determined that his army allowed that as a form of compensation, which was an abuse we tried to eliminate." The general went away unpunished, but the process sent a clear message. "The fact that this officer was called to account and had to face the commanding officer of the Stabilization Force with his career in jeopardy was not lost on the factions' senior politicians or their general officers."

In solitude, Meigs had worked out an effective solution to his problem. "In this dilemma," he says, "Grant showed me the way."

CHIP EDENS COMBINES the analytical with the spiritual to develop creative solutions as a leader. Chip is the rector of Christ Church Charlotte, where he leads a congregation of six thousand members. The church also has a staff of seventy people, a school, and numerous local and international partners for its social work. "Solitude has played a critical role in my journey as a leader," he says.

That journey began when Chip was thirteen, when he was a student at a military school. One day he paid a visit to the school's commandant. "Sir, with all due respect, the Sunday Assembly is a time when you're telling us what we've done wrong all week, and what we need to do next week. We're not getting a message of inspiration. You should hire a chaplain," Chip told him. The commandant responded, "Okay, if you want a chaplain, you do it. You execute it."

Chip went to see his pastor, telling him he didn't feel qualified to be a chaplain at the school. His pastor responded, "You are. You're being called. You should listen. You need to decide whether you want to be a leader this way." Chip now recalls, "I spent several days and nights reflecting on it, listening to a voice inside. Finally I decided to serve as chaplain at the school. That was when I began to use solitude to explore questions of the soul."

Chip went on to attend Yale Divinity School, from which he holds a master's degree. While he was there, he had an existential crisis. "I wasn't using my time well, and I didn't know what I wanted to do with my life." One day a friend invited Chip to a prayer service at five thirty A.M. the next day. Chip walked across a snowy campus that dark morning to a small stone chapel. "I figured there would be people praying aloud, that sort of thing. But there weren't. People were sitting there in candlelight, in stone silence." At first it was uncomfortable. "Sitting there in silence, I discovered how noisy my world was. Thoughts and emotions were constantly running through me." Chip likens his frame of mind then to a story about a Burmese monk. "One day a man came to the monk for advice. He started talking about all the problems in his life. The monk started pouring a cup of tea. The man kept talking, the monk kept pouring. The tea overflowed out of the cup, onto the table, onto the floor. The man said, 'Stop—what are you doing?' The monk replied, "Don't you see? This is you.'

"That was me then," Chip says. "Sitting in the silence of that chapel forced me to face what was running through me. There was so much noise, I almost left. I didn't want to face it. But I stayed, practicing deep breathing through the nose. Eventually I began to feel an inner peace. And I felt an intimacy with the people around me, even though I didn't know them. They were there for the same reason I was. I left feeling centered and refreshed."

Chip has continued his practice ever since. "Silence and solitude allows me to ground myself, to be conscious of what's going on inside me, what I'm feeling," he says. "Viktor Frankl wrote about how between every stimulus and response, there is a space. Silence and solitude creates a sacred space, an elongated space. The space gives you time to develop a creative response to what you're feeling. Otherwise there is only reaction."

Chip has refined his practice to include journaling. "I do journaling every single day," he says. His process itself is creative. "I have a stream of consciousness in my mind, thought streams. That gets a process going in my brain, which has an effect somewhere in my body or soul. It has a power over you. So the first thing I do is write down my thought streams. I name what I'm feeling. Then I engage it. I'm not judging it. I'm trying to understand it, why I'm feeling this way. Then I ask whether this feeling is something I want to bring back to my relationships. Anger and anxiety are not going to be part of a creative solution. Then I construct a response based on my values rather than on these feelings. And then I engage others with that response. It's a process of personal leadership."

Chip used this practice during a major leadership crisis at a church where he served years ago. "I was the number-two person there. It was a great big church, seven thousand members, a big staff, lots of local and international partnerships. A conflict developed regarding the church's direction. A group of parishioners tried to oust the church's board, its vestry. The dividers actually formed a 501(c)(3) organization to lobby the church's membership. It was full combat. People cut back on their giving; we were losing money. There was a lot of uncertainty about where we were going.

"I was very anxious, hyperfunctioning. Sometimes you have to hyperfunction; the enemy is coming after you, the bear is chasing you. But a hyperfunctioning leader can't listen, exercise judgment, navigate complexity. The neuropsychologists call it amygdala hijack." Chip's observations parallel those of Howard Prince.

"Leaders experience fear in times of turbulence or threat," Chip says. "You become obsessed about worst-case scenarios, fall into despair. That's the easiest way to resolve the conflict. That's when people snap—they quit the job, the marriage is ended, there's no hope. You need to step away from that and give yourself space to process it."

Yet Chip had stopped his practice of silence and solitude during this period. "That was one of the first things to go out the window when I started hyperfunctioning," Chip says. "Finally I went to see one of the monks I knew from my seminary days. He told me, 'Nothing can happen through you, until it happens inside you.' He told me to reconnect with silence and solitude."

Chip began his practice again. "Silence and solitude is most important in times like these. You need creativity. When you're being chased by a bear, it's hard to stop and invent the wheel, to find a better way to solve the problem. But you need to turn around and look at the bear—because it might not be a bear."

Through journaling, Chip began to work out a creative solution. "I thought, 'I'll address these people from a place of my values, what's real and true to me, a constructive response.'" One of Chip's core values is what he calls "community," which is very similar to what Karol Wojtyla (later Pope John Paul II) called "solidarity." "Community is a group of individuals who have made an inclusive commitment to support each other. Inclusive because they welcome others to join them." A healthy community can have differences, Chip says, but not division. "Differences are a product of ideas. Division is a product of behavior. A community means we live together with differences, but we can't be divided."

Chip's response to the crisis was centered on his idea of community. "I called the opposition leaders and asked them to sit with me in silence and solitude. They agreed. It was awkward at first, just like in the chapel at Yale. But there was that intimacy again. It showed them there was no physical or emotional threat. I began to create a community with them." Afterward, Chip says, "I asked them to think about their feelings, the effect their feelings were having on them, and the effect those feelings would have on our community and the organizations we served if the conflict continued. I was asking them to reflect the same way I had."

Then Chip engaged the church's leadership. "The process of silence and solitude, of engaging your feelings and exploring the reasons you're having them, also creates empathy with the people you're interacting with. You begin to understand how other people have these same feelings," he says. "I had some understanding of what the opposition group was feeling. So part of my response was to engage with our leaders and others in our congregation, to discuss who we are as a community, and how we could improve. It was true that we didn't have a plan for the future."

Ultimately, "the opposition group ran a separate slate of candidates for the vestry in an election. They were defeated. But I made sure they didn't see themselves as losers. Some left the church. Some stayed. Those who stayed experienced a degree of healing."

He sums up the experience. "The most important thing was that I engaged in silence and solitude to stay grounded. I could've been racked with anxiety. A leader needs to have presence, to show up to the moment grounded in one's self, as centered as one can be, ready to hear, to listen, to discern."

Chip's observations are poignant today. "A lack of silence and solitude leads to anxiety, which leads to demonization based on differences, which leads to conflict, which leads to violence. We need to reverse the flow. We need to invite people to think about their feelings, to address them, and then come up with a creative response that builds relationships and trust."

What we need, one might say, is grace.

CHAPTER 5

"Suppose We Were a Thing Intangible"
T. E. Lawrence, 1917

"Help comes from within, not from without."
—T. E. LAWRENCE

Intuition can give rise to not only clarity but creativity. For intuition can make connections not only between certain facts that usually come bundled together, but also between things that at first seem unrelated or even antagonistic. The fall of an apple, to cite a famous example from history, might seem to have nothing to do with astrophysics; but from such a fall, Sir Isaac Newton intuited an idea—the law of gravity—by which he explained the movement of planets in their orbits. (It seems no coincidence that Newton was resting quietly under a tree at the time.) And in the medical field, researchers have used various kinds of snake and spider venom—which normally bring certain bodily processes to a halt—to create medicines that slow those processes (cell growth or circulation, for example) when they spiral out of control. Intuition, in these instances, unlocks creativity by making connections no one has made before.

Intuition can also serve creativity in another way. Just as intuition can alert us that circumstances fit a certain pattern, so too it can alert us that a pattern that should be present is not. A simple example is that, if we encounter absolute stillness upon entering a room where normally there is a hum of background noise, we know that something is wrong. More to the point, conventional thinking rests on certain assumptions, namely that certain facts exist. Those facts themselves form a pattern; and based on those assumed facts, certain rules of decision follow. Meteorologists, for example, assume that the jet stream will follow a certain path, and make their predictions accordingly. But intuition can tell us when part of the pattern is missing, and thus that conventional thinking no longer works. During World War I, for example, the invention of the tank—which, unlike men, is relatively impervious to small-arms fire—foretold the end of days when an army could defend its position by means of soldiers firing rifles and machine guns from a trench. Winston Churchill (then First Lord of the Admiralty) grasped this fact sooner than the Germans did, and so the British gained an advantage.

Thomas Edward Lawrence ("of Arabia," as he is better known) used intuition in both of these ways in 1917, during the Arab Revolt. Lawrence's intuition came not from a consistent practice of solitude (though he craved it), but from a single episode, while he was laid up with dysentery for ten days in a tent. The results would change the history of his time and ours.

T. E. LAWRENCE WAS not a natural leader of men. As introverted as Eisenhower was extroverted, Lawrence wrote that "in all my life objects had been gladder to me than persons, and ideas than objects." His natural grain was not to lead men but to observe them—keenly, silently, insightfully, with a novelist's eye and command of lyrical prose. Ideas, not men, were his medium. "So the duty of succeeding with men," he wrote, "of disposing them to any purpose, would be doubly hard to me." Making his task even harder was the physical medium in which he operated: the naked desert of Arabia. "A weariness of the desert was always living in company, each of the party hearing all that was said and seeing all that was done by the others day and night." There his "craving for solitude" usually went unmet: "We had no shut places to be alone in, no thick clothes to hide our nature. Man in all things lived candidly with man." But for ten days in March 1917—while sick in a tent—Lawrence did find solitude. When he emerged, this physically small man, whose nature was to withdraw into the world of his own ideas, became a leader who decisively changed the course of events around him.

Those events were the Arab Revolt, in which the scattered tribes of Arabia eventually gathered together in opposition to their Turkish rulers. The revolt began in June 1916 at the direction of Emir Hussein bin Ali, leader of the Hashemite tribe and religious leader (or sharif) of the Islamic holy cities of Mecca and Medina. By then Turkey had allied itself with Germany in the Great War, and the British had promised Hussein money and equipment in support of the emir's struggle against their common enemy. At the revolt's outset, with the advantage of surprise, Hussein's tribesmen had quickly taken Mecca, which was defended by a small Turkish force. But the tribesmen had been completely repulsed in their efforts to take Medina, whose garrison numbered ten thousand. Meanwhile the British were slow to provide the promised support, claiming they needed a better understanding of conditions on the ground before they could intervene. To that end, Lawrence volunteered to travel from the coastal city of Jeddah inland to the battle zone.

In some respects Lawrence was a dubious choice for the role: he was a junior officer, had no formal military training, and was openly disdainful of military culture. But Lawrence was fluent in Arabic and deeply versed in Arabic tribal culture. After his sophomore year at Oxford, he spent the summer surveying Crusader castles in Syria. He returned to Syria the following year, just before Christmas 1910, and spent most of the next three years at an archaeological site at Carchemish, supervising laborers from various Arab tribes. In January 1914, he began a two-month survey of the Sinai Peninsula, during which he mapped the area surrounding the strategically important port of Akaba. His later work as an intelligence officer in Cairo also made him uniquely knowledgeable regarding the location of Turkish forces in Arabia. And Lawrence himself was a man of talents so formidable as to approach genius. A portrait artist described him shortly after the war:

> I have never seen so little employment or wastage of physical energy. The wide mouth smiled often, with humor and pleasure, sometimes extending to an unusual curve upward at the corners, a curious menacing curve, warning of danger ... The eyes roamed round, above, and might rest on mine or rather travel through mine, but never shared my thoughts, though noting them all ... These crystal eyes were almost animal, yet with a complete human understanding.

The artist also described Lawrence as he retreated into solitude: "At moments of thought, when he would ignore the presence of others, retiring into himself, [the eyes] would diverge slightly. Then, he was alone, and as inscrutable as a lion or a snake."

Thus, in October 1916, Lawrence journeyed alone toward the heart of the revolt. He had his own agenda as he did so. By then the revolt had settled into a stalemate, "which, with an irregular war," Lawrence believed, "was a prelude to disaster." The problem, Lawrence thought, was the absence of a critical ingredient from the rebellion's leadership: "not intellect, nor judgement, nor political wisdom, but the flame of enthusiasm, that would set the desert on fire." And so Lawrence's object—out of all proportion to his modest rank in the British Army—"was mainly to find the yet-unknown master-spirit of the affair, and measure his capacity to carry the revolt to the goal that I had conceived for it." The goal that Lawrence had conceived, moreover, was shared by none of his superiors. In October 1916, the Arab Revolt was confined to the Hejaz, a roughly two-hundred-mile swath of desert hills, peaks, and valleys (most of which lies in Jordan and Saudi Arabia today) that runs along the coast of the Red Sea, from Akaba in the north down past Mecca in the south. But Lawrence envisioned an Arab state that reached farther north, to Damascus and then up to Aleppo, to encompass not only the Hejaz but all of the

Arab-speaking peoples of Syria. His goal, known only to himself, was for the Arabs throughout this area to win their independence by their own arms, so that they would not lose it to British and French imperialism afterwards.

The revolt's "master-spirit," Lawrence knew, could not be the emir himself, for he was too old to lead action in the field. So Lawrence sought out and observed Hussein's four sons. The oldest, Abdulla, was the rebellion's presumptive leader. But Lawrence thought him a charlatan, who "affected openness" and was charming to the point of insincerity. He seemed a sybarite too, soft in body and spirit from the pleasures of his privileged station. The youngest, Zeid, was a mere "lad of nineteen, calm and flippant, no zealot for the revolt." The second-oldest, Ali, was "dignified and admirable" but also naïve, "without great force of character, nervous, and rather tired."

That left the third son, Feisal ibn Hussein, whom Lawrence met near the front lines of the revolt. Feisal, not Abdulla, had led most of the fighting so far. A sublime, ascetic figure, Feisal was a contrast in every way to Abdulla. Lawrence observed Feisal as "very tall and pillar-like, very slender, in his long white silk robes and his brown head-cloth bound with a brilliant scarlet and gold cord." His large eyes were "dark and appealing," his cheeks hollow, his bearing regal yet with a "hint of frailty." In mediating disputes among the fractious tribes joined to his command, Feisal "showed a mastery of tact, with a real power of disposing men's feelings to his wish." He "seemed to govern his men unconsciously: hardly to know how he stamped his mind on them, hardly to care whether they obeyed. It was great art; and it concealed itself, for Feisal was born to it." Feisal was the prophet Lawrence had sought; the aim of his trip was fulfilled.

To this man Lawrence now found himself attached, for the British threw their support behind Feisal and sent Lawrence back as an adviser to him. On the very night of his return, however, Lawrence found Feisal in the midst of disaster. The Turks had found an opening in the Arab lines and sent Feisal's tribesmen in a panic back to the rebellion's base in the southern coastal city of Yenbo.

The basic problem, Lawrence realized, was the difference in character between the Arab and Turkish soldiers. The tribesmen's strength was defense; a handful of Arab snipers in a rocky pass could hold hundreds of Turks at bay indefinitely. But the Arabs could not bear the crash of artillery among them, and a hundred entrenched Turks could repulse a thousand tribesmen with ease. Yet the rebellion's goal was to destroy the ten-thousand-man Turkish garrison at Medina; and thus, since the tribesmen's opening success at Mecca, the revolt had experienced little but defeat.

In March 1917, however, Lawrence suffered one of history's more consequential bouts of dysentery. After several days he was incapacitated, which sent him alone to his tent for ten days. And there his intuition came to the fore. For months Lawrence had observed the events of the revolt, which until then had been guided by "suitable maxims on the conduct of modern, scientific war"—the conventional thinking of his day. Those maxims assumed that "the aim of war" was "the destruction of the armed forces of the enemy." That assumption was valid in France, but not in Arabia; for the Arabs' goal "was geographical, to extrude the Turk from all Arabic-speaking lands in Asia . . . If they would go quietly the war would end." Lawrence now realized that the maxims of conventional military thought—the pattern of assumptions upon which they were based—"did not fit, and it worried me."

A hallmark of creativity is to reject conventional norms when they outpace their purpose, and that is exactly what Lawrence did in his deliberations alone. Having identified an "alternative end" of the Arabs' war—to eject the Turks rather than destroy them—Lawrence now reconsidered the Arabs' position. Notwithstanding the rebellion's setbacks, he thought, "it dawned on me that we had already won the Hejaz war." The enemy sought to hold an area of perhaps 140,000 square miles; "how would the Turks defend all that?" They could surely do so "by a trench line at the bottom," Lawrence thought, if the Arabs "came like an army with banners." But those were the means of traditional warfare, whose aim was to destroy the enemy; and now Lawrence began to consider alternative means. The Turks could not remain in Arabia without supplies sent to them via the Hejaz railway; thus, the Arabs needed merely to cut their lines of supply. The remaining question was how.

Here again Lawrence intuited an answer. In doing so he created the concept of insurgency, for his time and long after: "Suppose we were (as we might be) an influence, an idea, a thing intangible, invulnerable, without front or back, drifting about like a gas?" In Arabia "space was greater than the power of armies." The Arabs could "develop a habit of never engaging the enemy," instead materializing to strike where the Turks did not expect it, and then vanishing as quickly as they came. "In railway-cutting it would usually be an empty stretch of rail; and the more empty, the greater the tactical success." To defend against that threat, in a "vast unknown desert," the Turks would "need a fortified post every four square miles," each manned by at least twenty men, 160,000 in total—more than the Turks could muster. Meanwhile, lit by the flame of Feisal's leadership, his men would proselytize among the population the idea of an independent Arabic state—thus augmenting their own force while wearing down that of the enemy. "Final victory seemed certain," Lawrence concluded, if only they had the patience to wait for it.

Lawrence acted upon his vision soon after emerging from his tent. For the revolt to spread north of the Hejaz into Syria, he knew, the Arabs would need to seize the town of Akaba, on the Red Sea at the northern tip of the Hejaz. Lawrence also knew from mapping the area in 1914 that a sea-based attack on Akaba was hopeless. Landing troops there would be easy enough; but behind the city was the Wadi Itm, a rocky, winding, cliff-lined valley (a wadi is a dry valley or watercourse that contains water only after heavy rains), throughout which the Turks had strong fortifications from which they could shell the town. The wadi itself ran 25 miles, rising more than 4,000 feet, until finally reaching a plain that ran 20 miles to a railroad station at Maan. No force that landed at Akaba, therefore, could maintain its position there. Meanwhile, behind Maan, to the east, lay hundreds of square miles of the most forbidding desert in all of Arabia. No army could travel through there. By conventional measures, then, Akaba was unassailable.

But the strategy that Lawrence had developed in solitude was not conventional. Lawrence's plan was to journey 200 miles northeast of Wejh, into the heart of the desolation east of Maan, and there rally a tribal force that would travel another 100 miles northwest and then loop southwest another 150 miles to Maan, from whence they would fall upon the Turkish defenses in the Wadi Itm from the rear—an inland journey of 600 miles, all to capture a town "within gunfire of our ships." The Turks would never expect an attack from that direction. Lawrence wrote that his plan "was so entirely in the spirit of my sick-bed ruminations that its issue might well be fortunate, and surely would be instructive."

Lawrence's plan soon became reality. As he sat with Feisal in his tent one afternoon, one of Feisal's staff came in and whispered in his ear. Feisal then turned to Lawrence "with shining eyes, trying to be calm, and said, 'Auda is here.'" Auda was a renowned warlord from the Howeitat tribe in the Wadi Sirhan, through which Lawrence would travel per his plan. Immediately Lawrence was deeply impressed by him. "He must be nearly fifty now (he admits forty) . . . but he is still tall and straight, loosely built, spare and powerful, and as active as a much younger man." Married twenty-eight times and wounded thirteen, Auda had killed seventy-five Arabs since 1900; "Turks are not counted by Auda when they are dead." But most important, under Auda's handling his tribesmen had become the best fighting force in western Arabia. These were men who could take Akaba. Lawrence shared his plan with Auda, who pronounced it feasible and agreed to join the expedition.

Lawrence and Auda then rode with just a few dozen tribesmen to the Wadi Sirhan, 250 miles away, where Auda rallied the Howeitat to their cause. From there they began the long journey southeast to Akaba. Their only serious resistance—apart from the exceedingly harsh conditions of the journey itself—came near Maan. There the Arabs routed a battalion of Turks in a cavalry charge, with Auda leading the way. (He nearly got himself killed in the process, as Lawrence reported later, "since two bullets smashed his field glasses, one pierced his revolver holster, three struck his sheathed sword, and his horse was killed under him. He was wildly pleased with the

whole affair.") In the Wadi Itm the Arabs found the Turkish fortifications largely undefended, since the Turks had planned to man
them with troops only in the event of a landing at Akaba. On
July 6, the Arabs took the city itself. Lawrence's superiors had no
idea he was anywhere near there.

Lawrence's "sick-bed ruminations" had proved a success. Thus
the legend of Lawrence of Arabia was born, and the Arab Revolt—
though not, as it turned out, the cause of Arab independence—was
directed toward final victory.

PART III

CHAPTER 6

Emotional Balance

On April 30, 1863, near Chancellorsville, Virginia, Joseph "Fighting Joe" Hooker, then commanding general of the Union Army of the Potomac, executed one of the greatest maneuvers in American military history: he marched some seventy thousand men ten miles west along the northern bank of the Rappahannock River, sent them across the river at Kelly's Ford, and then wheeled them back east within striking distance of the Confederate rear. General Robert E. Lee did not even know that Hooker's men were there, and now Lee's sixty thousand men were trapped between Hooker's seventy thousand men in Lee's rear and another sixty thousand Union troops in Lee's front. All Hooker had to do was crush Lee's forces between the overwhelming strength of Hooker's own, and the war would be nearly over. Hooker exulted in his success: swaggering among his men on May 1, he declared, "The rebel army is now the legitimate property of the Army of the Potomac." Yet Lee's exploits had made him larger than life in the eyes of Confederate and Union soldiers alike. After Hooker's first contact with Lee's forces, Hooker got rattled and pulled his men back to a defensive position; and when Lee took the initiative and struck hard at Hooker's flank, Hooker himself went to pieces. (His men eventually carried him from the battlefield on a stretcher.) Although Hooker's men still outnumbered Lee's by two to one, within days Hooker marched his men back toward Washington. Hooker had lost his emotional balance, and with it all the overwhelming advantages that lay before him.

A LEADER TAKES on forces larger than himself. When a leader has clarity and conviction about how to deal with those forces, he feels himself a match for them. The result is a sense of equanimity, of emotional balance; and it is precisely that balance, when joined with clarity of thought, that allows a leader to exercise his best judgment. For judgment is the process of weighing competing interests, and the leader who comes to that process with equanimity puts no emotional distortion of his own upon the scale.

But precisely because he takes on forces larger than himself, a leader's equanimity is often more fragile than he lets on. The path of leadership is rarely linear; and with every setback, and every unwelcome surprise, the shadow of adversity grows larger. Sometimes the leader can take the setbacks in stride: he might have anticipated them, or at least assumed there would be something like them, and thus built in a margin of error to deal with them. Those kinds of setbacks might only confirm the leader's confidence in his overall plan. But other times—when adversity shows up in earnest—the floor of a leader's assumptions might drop out altogether. And as his assumptions fall away, so too can the clarity and conviction that he brought to his task in the first place. He feels he has miscalculated, perhaps fundamentally. During these moments—of quiet desperation in some cases, of panic all around in others—a leader feels the whole power and scope of what he is up against. The opposing forces again seem bigger than he is; and now they have slipped beyond his control. It is then—when a leader needs his judgment the most—that his equanimity is most jeopardized.

"AN EFFECTIVE LEADER is the person who can maintain their balance and reflect, when a lot of people around them are reacting," says James Mattis, a retired four-star Marine Corps General. He sees solitude as threatened today. "If I was to sum up the single biggest problem of senior leadership in the information age, it's a lack of reflection," he says.

The problem is one that General Mattis himself faced. Appointed in 2011 to succeed General David H. Petraeus as commander of United States Central Command, General Mattis oversaw American military operations in a region encompassing all of the Middle East—including Afghanistan, Iraq, Pakistan, and Iran. "With two wars on," he said then, "I get my solitude in smaller batches now." But still he made it a priority. Known as "the Warrior Monk," General Mattis brought his thousand-book library with him wherever he was stationed, leaving most of his personal effects behind. For him the books are portals to reflective solitude, their wisdom about the human condition oftentimes the starting place for sorting out the answer to a leadership problem. "The nature of man has not changed, unfortunately," he says. "And it's not going to change anytime soon.

"One source of a leader's strength comes from having some degree of reflective ability," General Mattis says. He cites Kipling's poem "If," which begins:

If you can keep your head when all about you
Are losing theirs and blaming it on you . . .

"Solitude allows you to reflect while others are reacting," he says. The leader who neglects to step out of the sweep of events, to contemplate from whence they came and where they might go, finds himself merely "blown from one thing to another." But the leader who steps outside events is a leader who can change them. "If you use solitude to draw on your reading and your past experience, to create some distance from what is happening around you immediately, then it's well used," he says. "We need solitude to refocus on prospective decision-making, rather than just reacting to problems as they arise. You have some external stimulus, then you go back to your experience, your education, and you see what needs to be done."

GENERAL MATTIS'S COMMENTS speak to maintaining emotional balance, as opposed to restoring it. Jaya Vadlamudi maintained her emotional balance when, as the senior communications officer for an international-relief organization, she deployed to Libya shortly after the fall of Moammar Gadhafi. Jaya is a native of New Jersey and holds a degree in international relations from Johns Hopkins University. After stints at Morgan Stanley and Sotheby's in New York, Jaya decided at age thirty to move to Los Angeles. "I didn't know anyone there," she says. "I just wanted to try something different. I resolved to try L.A. for at least a year." Now she has been there more than five years, working in the nonprofit sector.

One source of emotional turbulence for leaders is not so much the arrival of unexpected adversity, but simply a sense of being overwhelmed by a tangled mass of goals, obstacles, and inputs. "I use solitude to regain a sense of control," Jaya says. "There are so many inputs today, especially with smartphones. Often you don't have time to process it all. You need to make time to do that, to engage in a physical act that causes you to reflect." One of Jaya's practices is simply to write down her goals and the things she needs to do to meet them. "I'm big on list-making," she says. "I make lists of the things I've already done, and the things I want to accomplish." By identifying tasks and obstacles, Jaya cuts them down to size, thereby dispelling anxiety. "After I make a list, I think, 'Okay, I can do that.'"

Jaya used a variety of practices to maintain a sense of control while in Libya. "It was right after the civil war," she says. "The country hadn't seen democracy or outside help for decades. People were living in makeshift shelters; they couldn't get basic medical care. Every clinic had been looted or decimated." Jaya's organization had sent doctors and nurses to Libya before she arrived there. "My job was to put together videos to tell Westerners the stories of refugees who were caught in the middle of all the fighting. These people weren't terrorists. They were families who needed insulin or cancer medicine, babies being born, families just like us. We needed to humanize them and show the conditions they were living in."

Jaya's immediate task was to take photographs of the families her organization served, and also to interview them. Typically she would travel with two Libyan members of her organization to a village where one of the organization's doctors was providing services. "These were extremely remote villages, in the mountains," she says. "All stone, no trees or grass, small, old buildings." Usually there were long lines to see the doctor. "Nobody seemed upset by the lines," Jaya says. "The people were excited. Many of them hadn't seen a doctor for at least a year." Jaya would first ask the doctor about the situation in the village, which was often dire. "I saw people who had been injured in war, kids who were malnourished, kids with medical conditions." Then, through an interpreter, Jaya would talk with the families who were receiving medical care. "I would talk to them about what life was like before the war, and what their hopes were for their children. That was the beauty of the experience."

Yet the conditions of her work were extremely stressful. "It was a very unstable time," she says. "There were local militias in each village, teenaged boys or men in their twenties, holding machine guns. Everyone had weapons. Each village had a checkpoint. As we drove up to a checkpoint, we had no idea what we'd encounter. They'd look into the cars, ask why you were there. My organization had gotten me a local ID so that I wouldn't have to show anyone my American passport."

Compounding the stress was the fact that Jaya was a woman. "It was rare to see women in public there. You didn't see women strolling down the street, or girls playing outside. You might see some women at a market, or in line with their children for medical care. Otherwise women stayed inside the walls of their home. That wasn't because of Gadhafi. It was just the culture," she says. "Even the walls of the balconies were very high, so you couldn't see over them, and women couldn't be seen in their homes. That was hard for me to see." The situation affected Jaya directly. "When I applied for a visa, the form asked 'what male can speak for you.' The two options were 'husband' or 'father.' I had to set aside my reaction to that and just embrace where I was going." In the villages, Jaya says, "every inch of my skin was covered. I was surrounded by men. I tried to be very respectful and to stay completely quiet. We had to ask the permission of males to photograph the females. As a woman outside with the men, holding a big camera and wearing a giant backpack, I was a novelty to them. I felt vulnerable. It was scary to be an American woman there."

Jaya's relief came when she returned each night to a guesthouse alone. "That was my chance to breathe," she says. "It was a physical and emotional release, to take off the backpack and the headscarf. Then I could just be me. I would sit there and calm myself." Part of that process was similar to the process of meditation. "I would write in a journal about what I'd seen. What do I feel about this, what do I think about that. The process of writing would allow me to go deeper into my feelings. I would also roll my shoulders and neck on a tennis ball, thinking about the day, letting the thought streams go."

Apart from the physical and cultural stress of working in Libya, however, Jaya felt overwhelmed by all the information she was taking in. "I had all this wild data—things I'd seen and shoved away in my mind for later, photographs I'd taken, things I'd heard in the interviews. I had anxiety because I had all this stuff to get my arms around before I could execute my marketing mission when I got home. I was trying to make it discrete, to get a sense of control over it." Here as well the journaling was helpful: "I'd write down what I wanted to remember." But Jaya's photographs were the thing that assuaged all of her anxiety, personal and professional. "There was something very calming about just going through the images for the day. It would allow me to process what I'd seen. I was trying to whittle them down to the perfect frame. I was looking for a different kind of beauty. In Kenya, I had taken photographs of picturesque landscapes, a mother and baby looking into each other's eyes, or children playing outside. I didn't see that in Libya. What we did see was a doctor treating an entire family in a remote mountain town. The relief in their eyes—that was the beauty."

With that beauty came the reassurance that Jaya could execute her mission when she returned home. Jaya's time in the guesthouse each night gave her the sense of control over events—and thus the control over her own emotions—that she needed to face the day to come. "If

I didn't have that time alone," she says, "I wouldn't have been able to do that for long."

Katy Simonis likewise maintained her emotional balance by addressing her sources of tension as an Army platoon commander in Iraq. Katy graduated from West Point in 2003 and more recently earned an M.B.A. from the University of Chicago. In 2004 she was in al-Rashid, Iraq, which is a district in southern Baghdad. She had arrived in Iraq as an intelligence officer but longed for a chance to lead troops in the field. "Late one night," she says, "after we had completed our briefings, our Brigade Commander, a Colonel, called me into his office and said a platoon-leader position had opened in the 68th Chemical Company." The company was a mixed-gender unit whose mission initially was to search for nuclear, biological, and chemical weapons, but it had since been assigned the task of securing the area around al-Rashid. "Because we were in the middle of combat operations and 68th Chemical was a mixed-gender unit, the Brigade Commander had the author-ity to place whoever he felt was best suited in the open position, regardless of gender or specialty," she says. "He said he would arrange for me to interview for the position if I was interested. I was. I still feel so much gratitude that he took a chance and gave me the opportunity to grow as a young leader."

Soon Katy was commanding a platoon of fourteen soldiers who, unlike herself, had already been engaged in combat operations for five months. At the time, she was the only female platoon commander in the battalion, which comprised about a thousand soldiers. The platoon's jobs included looking for sources of enemy mortar and rocket attacks and conducting combat patrols on "Route Irish," a heavily traveled road running due south from Baghdad. "Our base was up against Route Irish," she says. "We had responsibility for some parts of Baghdad to the north of us, and some poor rural areas to the south. The area around the base was open." Each patrol included eleven soldiers, riding in at least three vehicles, each with at least one mounted machine gun. Katy would operate the machine gun as she led the patrol.

Katy says that her "biggest challenge as a young leader was the tension." A lot of the tension came during combat patrols, which were among the most hazardous missions conducted by soldiers in Iraq. "The main threat was IEDs," or improvised explosive devices—typically an artillery shell buried under the surface of a dirt road. When an American vehicle drove over the place where the shell was buried, an insurgent spotter would detonate it remotely, often using a cell phone. The insurgents wore civilian clothes and were often surrounded by civilians. "It was very difficult to tell what was a threat on patrol, and what wasn't," Katy says. Another threat was mortar fire, which sometimes landed on the base, and other times targeted American troops on patrol. "Our platoon was in the rotation to serve as a quick-reaction force, which meant we were on constant alert for a twenty-four-hour shift," she says. "We might get called out to deal with a vehicle stuck in the mud, or an overturned vehicle, or an unexploded mortar round or rocket sticking out of the ground somewhere. One time, the enemy knew we were coming, and they fired mortar rounds at the location when we got there."

But for Katy, much of the tension was more personal. "I was constantly aware that I was the least experienced member of the platoon, and the only female platoon commander," she says. "I felt like I was representing my entire gender. I wanted to do a great job." As a female platoon commander, Katy had her own room on the base. She used it, in General Mattis's words, "to refocus on prospective decision-making." Katy could do only so much about the tension of leading troops in combat; but during times alone in her room, she dealt with her other sources of tension by defining herself as a leader. One part of her identity as a leader was a willingness to ask questions. "You want to show you're in charge, but also that you're learning and don't know everything. Subordinates know that, as a new leader, you're inexperienced. I realized they'd rather have an inexperienced leader who's asking questions than one who isn't." Another part was a willingness to empower her soldiers. "I began having a junior sergeant co-lead patrols with me, so they would know what to do if something happened to the patrol leader," she says. "The only way to get that experience is to be that one person who's leading the patrol." Katy also set an example by taking her turn for days off from patrol. "As a leader you feel like you constantly have to be there, but I'd seen other platoon leaders burn out," she says. "A leader sets the tone for what's permissible. I wanted my subordinates to know that I thought periodic rest was important, so I did that myself. It gave them permission as well."

In the months that followed, Katy led her platoon in the execution of over a hundred combat patrols. "The solitude afforded by my own room gave me the time and space to process how each mission had gone and think through adjustments for future patrols," she says. "Focusing on the decisions I needed to make going forward helped to reassure me that I was doing everything I could to limit the danger to my troops. That helped to limit my anxiety as a leader."

THERE ARE TIMES when even the best leaders lose their emotional balance. Leadership brings with it responsibility, and responsibility, in times of serious adversity, brings emotional turmoil and strain. In this sense responsibility is like a lever, which can upset a leader's emotional balance when adversity presses down hard on one end. When the adversity is threatening enough or comes without warning, it can unbalance the leader at a single stroke. Even a leader as great as Lincoln was floored more than once in this way. Other times the effect is cumulative, coming after a period of sustained high tension—of pressure on one end and resistance on the other—until finally the leader's equanimity begins to give way. The point is that every leader has her emotional limits, and there is no shame in exceeding them. What distinguishes effective leaders from inferior ones, rather, is their ability to restore their emotional balance.

SOMETIMES THE QUICKEST way for a leader to restore her emotional balance, or at least begin to, is through catharsis. Katy Simonis used catharsis to restore her emotional balance on one occasion when her emotions were too great to hold in. Less than two weeks after she took over her platoon, she received news that a friend of hers from high school—a Marine stationed about ten miles south of Katy's base—had been terribly wounded in an IED attack while on patrol. "He died back in the States," Katy says. "He had recently sent me an e-mail asking if I would be going through his area of operations anytime soon, so that we could maybe meet up. After he died I frantically searched my in-box for that e-mail and realized I had never responded to him, which caused me deep regret."

For Katy the news about her friend came at a vulnerable time: she was a new platoon leader and was scheduled to go on one of her first combat patrols that day. Yet she decided not to go on that patrol. "I knew I needed a moment," she says. "I gave myself permission to take some time." She spent that afternoon alone in her room. "I knew if I didn't take time to process the event, I wouldn't be effective on patrol." After the first surge of emotion had run its course, Katy was able to focus again on her responsibilities as a leader. "I realized how precious life is, and how quickly it can be taken away. On patrol, you never know what will happen when you leave the gate. The loss of my friend made very real what was at stake in my leadership."

ANOTHER WAY FOR leaders to restore their emotional balance is through perspective. Pam Slim regained a sound sense of perspective during a family crisis in 2007. Pam is the author of two acclaimed books, *Escape from Cubicle Nation* and *Body of Work*, and operates her own executive-coaching firm, Ganas Consulting. She lives in Mesa, Arizona, with her husband, Darryl, and their two children.

Darryl operates his own construction business, which was thriving into early 2007. At that time Pam was writing *Cubicle Nation*, a book inspired by her experience of leaving a large corporation to start her own business. Very soon after the birth of their daughter in October 2007, however, Darryl's business began to suffer along with the national economy. "Almost overnight," Pam says, "the construction projects went away. Darryl's business had no income;

it was losing money." To compound matters, Darryl had recently expanded his business, buying new equipment and taking on debt. "It was terrifying because of the financial responsibility we'd taken on in his business," Pam says. "I would wake up at three A.M., wondering how we'd keep it all together." At the same time, "I was writing a book about how to start your own business. I felt like an imposter."

Pam describes herself as "hyperextroverted," while Darryl is a strong introvert. During this crisis he told her, "You need time alone." Darryl is Navajo, and her father-in-law shared with her a traditional Navajo teaching: "When you're out of sorts, sit on the earth. Connect with it."

She took their advice. Every morning, before the rest of the house was awake, Pam would sit on a particular rock behind her house and look out to the east, at the Superstition Mountains, as the sun rose. "I was connecting with nature," she says. "Looking at the mountains, I thought about how they'd been there a long time. Through all kinds of human experience, they were always there. I started to gain a clarity about what we were up against. It wasn't quite as big as I thought it was."

With that broader perspective, Pam says, "I began to let go of my fear." And as her fear gave way, her reflections became more positive. "I realized that we weren't alone. A lot of other construction firms were in the same trouble. I also reconnected with the mission of my book. I got my head on straight again." Pam's father told her that, because of the struggles she and Darryl were going through, she'd "write a better book" and "know more about the balance of starting a business." "I held on to that idea," Pam says.

"At the time, I didn't realize how important my time alone on that rock was to me," she says. "The biggest thing it gave me was perspective."

SANYIN SIANG OFFERS some refinements on the subject of perspective. Sanyin is executive director of the Coach K Center on Leadership and Ethics at Duke University. She also writes about leadership for the *Huffington Post*. "We need solitude during points of failure," she says. "With great leadership drive comes great risks and great successes, really high points and devastating low points. Both are emotional jolts."

Sanyin advocates what she calls "strategic reflection." The process enhances perspective not so much by measuring adversity against something larger, but by distilling the source of turmoil itself down to a smaller size. Like Chip Edens, the pastor who practices "silence and solitude," Sanyin says that "solitude allows you to examine why you're emotionally reacting a certain way. Strategic reflection allows you to see what's really important and what's a distraction. Sometimes what you're upset about is actually more of a distraction."

Dena Braeger—the West Point graduate and mother of six children in Texas—emphasizes the same point. "When I'm practicing solitude regularly, I self-correct so much better. I'm more focused on what's important, and I let things go that aren't important. I can hear my own voice." One of her relatives tends to make comments that are literal and direct. "Things like 'you look tired, you look terrible.' When I'm practicing solitude, these are things I can choose not to be offended by." But reflection also allows her to choose to take a stand about things that are important. "If I get into an argument, it's never in the heat of the moment. I think through my case in advance. I've decided to be upset."

Sanyin also advocates strategic reflection during times of leadership success, for two reasons. One is that, "after a big success, more stimuli can just go to your head." Just as during adversity a leader might think the situation is worse than it actually is, so too the leader who seeks out accolades and praise might think that his situation is better than it actually is. "Stepping away from those external stimuli can keep a leader grounded," Sanyin says. The second reason is related. "Without reflection, the chase for success is sometimes just vanity." Praise and attention are fleeting, and then gone. The leader is left feeling empty unless she authentically connects her success with a more lasting purpose. "For a long time, I wanted to be a contributor to a national publication," Sanyin recalls. "When I finally realized that goal, I felt elation for a day, and then empty. I needed reflection to realize what my goal was about: a platform to express a point of view that can make the world better. The chase was just vanity. Success brings emotional distractions just as failure does."

ANOTHER CONTRIBUTION OF solitude is more contemplative. Even good leadership sometimes brings hard consequences: lives lost, workers laid off, austerity where once there was largesse. Productive solitude allows a leader to reflect upon these realities of leadership, and thereby to reconcile himself with what has already happened and what may happen yet. (Mozart describes this process in his Piano Concerto no. 20 in D Minor, when he moves from the dark adversity of the first movement, to the sublime acceptance of the second.) The process is one of recognizing loss as an unavoidable reality of life. And that recognition, in turn, allows the leader to move forward again.

General Mattis emphasizes solitude's role in accepting the consequences of leadership. Combat, of course, brings the hardest of consequences. "What we do by incorporating violence into the human condition has an omnipresent moral aspect," General Mattis says. "Combat is an atavistic experience that can take you to an emotional place that you can never come out of. That is not necessarily a bad place. There's something called 'post-traumatic growth,' where you come out of the experience a more placid, gentle, positive person, who keenly appreciates every part of life."

The process is not limited to combat, and solitude can facilitate it, by helping the leader pass through the emotional rapids to reach the pool beyond. "There is a spiritual and emotional aspect to solitude," General Mattis says. "Solitude can bring an emotional contemplation that allows you to reconcile the human aspect with the more mechanical aspects of our actions, the things we're required to do. It brings you to a more balanced place to carry out the mission."

COAUTHOR MIKE ERWIN faced an emotional crisis after returning home in 2009 from a deployment to Afghanistan—his second, in addition to a deployment to Iraq in 2004, two years after he graduated from West Point. Mike was an intelligence officer; and beginning in 2006, while most of his counterparts were focused on Iraq, Mike focused on the insurgency in Afghanistan, particularly in the Helmand and Kandahar provinces. "I knew every valley, every tribe in Southern Afghanistan, what they were doing, how they were doing it, and why."

Mike's second deployment to Afghanistan began in January 2009, right after President Obama announced that American forces would begin a surge there. Now the focus of America's military effort would be on precisely the area that Mike knew best. Immediately Mike found himself leading a twenty-five-person intelligence group and working eighteen-hour days with a deep sense of purpose. The Marines were scheduled to surge into Helmand Province in late May, the Army into Kandahar two months later. "Helmand was a stronghold of the insurgency," Mike says. He pushed for a large-scale raid into the area before the Marines arrived in May, eventually making his case directly to the two-star general responsible for the area. The raid, called Operation Siege Engine, took place in May 2009. American forces seized massive amounts of munitions, and narcotics with a street value of hundreds of millions of dollars. "The operation put the Taliban off balance, gave the Marines some breathing room," Mike says. "It saved Marine lives."

But in June, just as the Afghan surge was getting underway, Mike received orders to return to the United States and attend graduate school at the University of Michigan. Afterward he would teach leadership at West Point for three years. Thus, after five years of deploying or preparing to deploy, Mike would now be stateside for five years.

The change was wildly disorienting for Mike. "In a twenty-four-hour period, I went from a combat zone to home, at Fort Bragg, in North Carolina. I didn't have time to process the change." The following month he and his wife, Genevieve, moved to Ann Arbor, where his sister Monica and her husband, Jonny Algor (another West Pointer), were living for the time being. Otherwise Mike knew no one there. Later that month he attended "orientation day" for Michigan's personality Ph.D. program. "I felt like I had made a big mistake. The students were mostly twenty-three to twenty-five years old with vastly differently life experiences from mine. They were there to learn about topics like sleep and romantic relationships. I was there to learn about positive psychology and post-traumatic growth. It was like being on a completely different planet."

Mike soon found himself in an emotional spiral, overwhelmed by guilt about being on a college campus while his military friends were fighting in the Afghan surge. "August through October was a terrible time in Afghanistan," he says. "The Army's KIA—killed in action—were insanely high in Kandahar, mostly from IEDs." Mike was distraught about the casualties, because that spring he had done everything he could to warn incoming senior officers about the IED threat. "I gave them a stern talking-to about it. I told them, 'This isn't like it was in Iraq. You can't drive vehicles in Kandahar province! You have to dismount and walk.'"

Mike tried to assuage his frustration and guilt by doing everything he could from Ann Arbor to help the effort in Afghanistan. A few months earlier, before Mike left Afghanistan, General David Petraeus had sent him an e-mail, saying that he had heard that Mike had been ordered to attend graduate school and that Mike had "a good command of what's going on in Southern and Western Afghanistan." General Petraeus concluded, "Let's find a way to keep you engaged in this mission when you have time." Mike threw his energies into that effort, reading reports about the Taliban early in the morning and late at night, and sending hundreds of e-mails to friends and mentors deployed there.

In January 2010, Mike came up with the idea of reuniting his military friends and raising money for a prominent veterans' organization at the Minnesota Twin Cities Marathon, scheduled for October 3 that year. Mike recruited about sixty friends and colleagues from around the country to participate. To add to Mike's frustrations, however, the veterans' organization said they would not fly any of their veteran beneficiaries to the event. Mike then started thinking about starting his own nonprofit to support veterans.

Around that same time, Mike began a practice of going on long runs near his home in Scio Township, Michigan. Mike's neighborhood bordered farm country, and each day he would run out of his subdivision, turn right onto a dirt road, cross a small bridge over a creek, and then run past the cornfields for miles on end. There, in silence save for the occasional passing car, Mike left the tumultuous events of his life behind him—and with them the e-mails, texts, and Facebook posts.

At first Mike's purpose was to train for the Twin Cities Marathon. But the runs became more than training for Mike. "Running is cheaper than therapy," he says. "I engaged in a lot of self-talk on the runs. It's cognitively impossible to have that kind of self-dialogue with inputs coming in from other people." He thought, "During the next five years, I know I'm going to hear about friends and people I know who are killed or wounded in Afghanistan. I can't go back there to do anything about it. That's not possible. Forget about what I can't do there. What can I do to make a difference here?"

In the weeks that followed, during dozens of hours running on dirt roads past the cornfields, Mike began to flesh out his idea of starting his own nonprofit organization to support veterans. "What if we focused on marathons and triathlons as a way to raise funds for returning veterans, and then used the funds to build relationships with them?" With nothing but an idea, on March 23, 2010, Mike filed the IRS paperwork for his new nonprofit, which he named Team Red, White & Blue, known as Team RWB.

Yet Mike had more emotional turmoil to come. At first he simply had a case of founder's remorse, wondering, "What the hell am I doing starting my own nonprofit?" He also ran into the typical adversity that a new organization faces. "When you try to find support for any nonprofit in year one," he says, "people tell you, 'You're irrelevant, no one knows who you are, someone else is already serving that need.'" But those setbacks were modest compared to what Mike felt in April 2010, when his unit deployed back to Afghanistan. "All my progress with rationalizing why it was okay for me to be back here was erased," he says. "I found myself thinking, 'Can I take a year off from school and deploy?' But I couldn't. I had orders to be here, and my wife had just had our first child."

In June came an event that condensed all of Mike's feelings into a burst of emotion. On a local Ann Arbor website, Mike read that Captain Joel Gentz, an Air Force pararescueman from the next town over, had been killed in action in Helmand Province on June 10. Mike was a captain himself then. "I had never met Joel, but I certainly knew men like him," Mike says. "Pararescuemen had put their lives on the line for some Green Berets in my last deployment." That a young man with the same rank as Mike, from nearly the same town, had been killed in a place Mike knew so well, while Mike himself was in graduate school, brought back an overwhelming sense of guilt.

On the day of Joel's memorial service, Mike put on his formal Army Greens and drove to the neighboring town of Grass Lake, Michigan. There he stood in the receiving line, sweating in the hot sun in his woolen uniform, waiting to offer his condolences to Joel's parents. "When my time came to speak to them, time seemed to stand still," Mike says. "I admitted to them that I hadn't known Joel, and said I was so sorry for their loss."

Mike found himself crying uncontrollably on the drive home. Once he got there, he laced up his shoes and went on a long run. "I was feeling more than thinking," he says. "But the one thought that fixed in my head was a sense of determination to make Team RWB into something that helped veterans who did make it home."

Just as catharsis is a process of purging emotion, sublimation is a process of channeling emotion toward something positive. Mike was engaged in sublimation then, thinking furiously during his long runs about ways to get Team RWB off the ground. He also decided to dedicate a Team RWB event to Joel, and to hold it in Michigan so that Joel's family could attend. Yet for Mike the healing process was not linear. In August 2010, he learned through an e-mail that his darkest predictions had come true: two of the best soldiers he had served with during his last tour, Master Sergeant Dave Smith and Sergeant First Class Mark Holbert, had struck an IED while driving in Helmand Province. Dave lost an arm in the blast; Mark lost both legs and was fighting for his life, though he would survive.

Guilt and grief became one for Mike in the summer of 2010. But his process of sublimation allowed him to heal. During by now hundreds of hours of runs, first past cut, brown stalks of last year's corn, then past new-planted rows, and then past tall green stalks swaying in the wind, Mike channeled his emotions toward something positive. If he could not help his comrades while they were in Afghanistan, he would help them when they came home. And only then could Mike finally make peace with himself. "I did all I could for the guys coming in after me," he thought to himself on a run. "I did my part."

Team RWB's inaugural event was the Twin Cities Marathon on October 3. Hundreds of supporters flew in from all over the country. On October 15, Mike ran in the Joel Gentz Memorial fifty-four-mile ultramarathon, taking turns carrying an American flag all the way from Pontiac, Michigan, to downtown Detroit. Out of the emotional trauma of the past fifteen months, Mike had found growth, and with it a chance to help tens of thousands of his former colleagues and friends. Team RWB now has approximately 140,000 members and more than two hundred chapters across the country.

"People will tell you why you should feel better about your actions," Mike says. "But the only way you can reach that conclusion is on your own."

CHAPTER 7

Acceptance
Abraham Lincoln, 1863

"Your golden opportunity is gone, and I am distressed immeasurably because of it."

—ABRAHAM LINCOLN, JULY 14, 1863

Excess emotion—emotion beyond a leader's own limits to control—has to go somewhere. A leader can bottle up the emotion for a while, as Ulysses S. Grant sometimes did. But the leader who thinks he can cram it down indefinitely is only deluding himself; the emotion will either distort his judgment or eventually paralyze him altogether, as it did Hooker.

A more effective leader is honest with himself about the source of his excess emotion and about the need to dissipate it in a benign way. He will, of course, be careful about doing that publicly: in a crisis his subordinates are likely to be emotional too, and the sight of their leader's fear may act as an accelerant to their own. Or they might lose faith in a leader who appears overmatched by events. The solution, then, is to do what successful leaders have done in crises throughout history: make a choice to go somewhere and break down in private. Productive solitude, in this instance, is simply a pressure-relief valve for leaders who are willing to acknowledge their own limitations.

But in these situations productive solitude can do more than that for a leader. In leadership, as in other areas of life, one's anxiety about an event is sometimes out of proportion to the event itself. When adversity is viewed close-up, as it breaks upon the scene, it often seems larger and more overwhelming than it truly is. In those moments neither the leader nor anyone else can see past it.

When adversity fills the windshield, it is time to change one's perspective. Productive solitude allows a leader to make that change. By removing herself from the clamor around her, the leader can step outside events, to see them in a larger context—and thereby see their limitations. By cutting the problem down to size intellectually, the leader does the same thing emotionally. Then she can shift her focus away from fear and recrimination, and toward the real tasks of positive leadership: action, goals, and the preparation of plans to meet them. The point reaches back to the first sentence of the introduction to this book: to lead others, you must first lead yourself. The leader who encounters a serious crisis and successfully manages his emotional balance throughout it does precisely that.

ON JULY 14, 1863, only eleven days after the Union's victory at Gettysburg and only ten after Grant's pivotal conquest of Vicksburg, Abraham Lincoln suffered what was likely his most painful setback as commander in chief during the Civil War. At Gettysburg, Lee had been forced to relinquish the battlefield for the first time, his Army of Northern Virginia reduced by almost twenty-three thousand men. At that moment Lee was more vulnerable than ever before. Heading south on the evening of July 3, just hours after the final, shattering failure of Pickett's Charge, Lee's remaining troops were in enemy country, disoriented by defeat, and without reinforcements or ammunition to fight anything near a sustained battle. The Union's commanding general, George Meade, and his exhausted but more numerous troops followed behind. Lee's objective was a Confederate pontoon bridge at Williamsport, Maryland, over which his soldiers would cross the

Potomac River into the refuge of Virginia. But Union cavalry would destroy the bridge long before Lee got there, and meanwhile there began a summer rain that would continue unrelenting for nearly ten days. By the time Lee reached the Potomac the river was impassable, even its shallowest, rocky stretches now swollen with surging brown waters. For more than a week, Lee and his depleted army would be trapped there.

Lincoln immediately grasped the opportunity before him. Meade's forces had surrounded Lee's in a semicircle at the water's edge. Coming close on the heels of Grant's capture of an entire Confederate army in the West—more than thirty thousand men—the destruction of Lee's army in the East could end the war at a single stroke. For Lincoln, especially, the magnitude of the opportunity must have been excruciating. More than any other wartime president, before or since, Lincoln absorbed into his emotional recesses the war's human cost. In this respect he was singularly without defenses. As Doris Kearns Goodwin observes, Lincoln "possessed extraordinary empathy—the gift or curse of putting himself in the place of another, to experience what they were feeling, to understand their motives and desires." She notes further: "He was uncommonly tenderhearted. He once stopped and tracked back half a mile to rescue a pig caught in the mire—not because he loved the pig," but just to take the "'pain out of his own mind.'" For more than two years, however, Lincoln had borne the pain of hundreds of thousands of men killed and maimed, and of even more parents and widows and orphans bereaved—all of it caused by a war that Lincoln himself insisted must continue. Now, with Lee trapped, Lincoln saw a Providential opportunity to bring the nation's suffering, and his own, to an abrupt end.

But Meade hesitated. Lincoln's anxieties began to escalate when he read Meade's congratulatory order to his troops at Gettysburg: "Our task is not yet accomplished, and the commanding general looks to the army for greater efforts to drive from our soil every vestige of the presence of the invader." Upon reading it, Lincoln cried out: "Drive the invaders from our soil! *Great God! Is that all?*" (Lincoln was also annoyed by the reference to "our soil." To his personal secretary John Hay, Lincoln said: "Will our Generals never get that idea out of their heads? The whole country is *our* soil.") Lincoln sought to focus Meade upon the opportunity before him: through an intermediary, Lincoln telegraphed Meade that, if he could complete "the literal or substantial destruction of Lee's Army, the rebellion will be over." For several days, however, Meade took no action, instead telegraphing back reports about mud, his men's exhaustion, and the strength of Lee's defenses. During this time, according to the telegraph officer in the War Department, Lincoln's "anxiety seemed as great as it had been during the battle itself." He "walked up and down the floor, his face grave and anxious, wringing his hands and showing every sign of deep solicitude." Soon Lincoln tried a different approach, sending Meade an off-the-record dispatch (never found, but attested to by Lincoln's eldest son, Robert Todd Lincoln, among others), which stated: "You will follow up and attack Genl. Lee as soon as possible before he can cross the river. If you fail this dispatch will clear you from all responsibility and if you succeed you may destroy it." Lincoln's spirits rose briefly on July 11: Hay wrote in his diary then that "the President seemed in a specially good humor today, as he had pretty good evidence that the enemy were still on the North side of the Potomac and Meade had announced his intention of attacking them in the morning." But Meade did not attack on the twelfth, or the thirteenth. Finally, on the morning of the fourteenth, Meade moved forward to begin the climactic battle—only to find that Lee's men had crossed the river just hours before.

By all accounts the effect upon Lincoln was devastating. Hay wrote that day that "the Prest was deeply grieved." A journalist who saw him that afternoon said that Lincoln's "grief and anger were sorrowful to behold." To his Secretary of the Navy, Gideon Welles, Lincoln exclaimed: "What does it mean, Mr. Welles? Great God! What does it mean?" Welles added in his diary that day: "On only one or two occasions have I ever seen the President so troubled, so dejected, and discouraged." Even Lincoln's Treasury Secretary, Salmon P. Chase—whose ceaseless machinations to obtain the Presidency for himself in 1864 made him perhaps the most aggravating person ever to hold Cabinet rank—wrote the following day that Lincoln "was more grieved and indignant than I have ever seen him."

And yet only five days later, on July 19, Hay wrote in his diary: "The Tycoon [i.e., Lincoln] was in very good humour." Good enough, in fact, that Lincoln composed a lighthearted doggerel that morning about how Lee had "skedaddled back" to Virginia. So the question arises: given the magnitude of the setback Lincoln had just experienced, how did he recover his emotional balance so quickly?

We do not know exactly what Lincoln did, hour by hour, during those five days of recovery. But we do know that he did two things, both cathartic, and both alone. One was that he retreated to his bedroom and wept. Robert Todd Lincoln went there, later on the fourteenth, and found his father "in tears, with head bowed upon his arms resting on the table at which he sat."

The other was that Lincoln wrote a letter to Meade. It began on a conciliatory note: "I am very—_very_ grateful to you for the magnificent success you gave the cause of the country at Gettysburg, and I am sorry now to be the author of the slightest pain to you." But only two sentences later, Lincoln put into words his frustrations of the past ten days:

> I had been oppressed nearly ever since the battles at Gettysburg, by what appeared to be evidences that yourself, and Gen. Couch, and Gen. Smith, were not seeking a collision with the enemy, but were trying to get him across the river without another battle . . . The case, summarily stated, is this. You fought and beat the enemy at Gettysburg; and, of course, to say the least, his loss was as great as yours. He retreated; and you did not, as it seemed to me, pressingly pursue him; but a flood in the river detained him, till, by slow degrees, you were again upon him. You had at least twenty thousand veteran troops directly with you, and as many more raw ones within supporting distance, all in addition to those who fought with you at Gettysburg; while it was not possible that he had received a single recruit; and yet you stood and let

the flood run down, bridges be built, and the enemy move away at his leisure, without attacking him.

In the next paragraph, Lincoln described the lost opportunity and his own reaction to it:

> Again, my dear general, I do not believe you appreciate the magnitude of the misfortune involved in Lee's escape. He was within your easy grasp, and to have closed upon him would, in connection with our other late successes, have ended the war. As it is, the war will be prolonged indefinitely . . . Your golden opportunity is gone, and I am distressed immeasurably because of it.

A vindictive superior would have sealed the letter and promptly sent it to a subordinate who had caused him such distress. But Lincoln simply filed it away, writing upon the envelope, "never sent or signed." His purpose in writing it, he likely knew all along, was not to communicate with Meade—any more than weeping in his room was.

Doris Kearns Goodwin again observes, in connection with a lesser crisis, that "Lincoln's ability to retain his emotional balance in such difficult situations was rooted in an acute self-awareness and an enormous capacity to dispel anxiety in constructive ways." Self-awareness is an asset earned through introspection; and Lincoln used it here to seek out the solitude of his own room and later to write a letter he knew he would never send. In doing so, he accomplished at least two things. The first was to give passage to the great emotion that had seized him when he learned of Lee's escape. That emotion unbalanced Lincoln as it would anyone, rendering him for the time being unable to function effectively as a leader. It would have been foolish for Lincoln to remain at his post every moment that day—though many leaders, less introspective and more inclined to see themselves as continuously indispensable, would have done that. Lincoln's wisdom was to step outside the day's events and let his emotions run their course, in the privacy of his bedroom. He then continued that process by expressing his frustrations—fully, precisely, and unflinchingly—in the unsent letter to Meade. When Lincoln emerged from that process, he controlled his emotions more than they controlled him.

A second benefit, again central to Lincoln's recovery of his emotional balance, was the recovery of his perspective. When the news of Lee's escape first hit, it was for Lincoln an oceanic mass of adversity: "What does it mean, Mr. Welles? Great God! What does it mean?" By writing his letter to Meade, however, Lincoln began the process of defining what it meant. Alone with his pen, Lincoln defined not for Meade—he never read the letter—but for himself, "the magnitude of the misfortune involved in Lee's escape": that the war would not end anytime soon, but would "be prolonged indefinitely." That misfortune was very large indeed, especially for a president as emotionally vulnerable to the war's toll as Lincoln was. By the end of the letter, however, Lincoln had regained his perspective. He says that the war would be "prolonged," but not that it might be *lost*—and until only two weeks before, there remained the very real possibility that it would be lost. Events at Gettysburg and Vicksburg had made that possibility much more remote. Lincoln had stepped outside his adversity, to study it within his own mind—and by doing so he drew boundaries around it. That allowed him to place the adversity in context, thereby restoring his perspective—and with it his emotional balance.

From there, Lincoln only had to reach back to the points that had sustained him from the war's outset. As he put them four months later: "that this nation, under God, shall have a new birth of freedom—and that government of the people, by the people, for the people, shall not perish from the earth."

Lincoln never discounted the magnitude of the opportunity lost when Lee escaped. But soon his magnanimity returned to the fore. Within days, Lincoln recognized that the obstacles in Meade's way—his troops, too, had just fought an epic battle—were greater than Lincoln had appreciated before July 14. (Lincoln never saw those obstacles to be anywhere near commensurate, however, with the opportunity that lay beyond them.) On July 21, Lincoln sent a letter to another general—who Lincoln surely knew would hand over the letter to Meade—in which he balanced a more measured expression of disappointment at Lee's escape with the statement that "I am profoundly grateful for what was done, without criticism for what was not done." He closed with his usual generosity: "Gen. Meade has my confidence as a brave and skillful officer, and a true man."

By early August, Lincoln was fully himself again. "I have rarely seen him more serene & busy," wrote Hay on August 7. "The Tycoon is in fine whack."

CHAPTER 8

Catharsis
Ulysses S. Grant, 1864

"The leader who is placid inside is much more formidable in battle."

—GENERAL JAMES MATTIS

Cleaning up the wreckage after a storm is one thing; living through the storm as it happens, with its fury still a living force and its damage still uncertain, is another. Leadership during a crisis presents different challenges than leadership after its consequences have already arrived. During a crisis, a leader faces not distress about what has already happened, but fear about what might. Much of that fear will be his own, but even more will be around him, in his subordinates, some of whom might urge the leader to be more fearful than he already is. The leader will also feel the shocks and jolts of the crisis itself as it unfolds; and as he navigates his way through it, the weight of his responsibility will feel heavier than at any other time.

Moments like these are among the loneliest for a leader. Yet they are also the most difficult in which to find solitude. When a gale strikes, a leader's place is not belowdecks, but at the helm. He should strive to maintain a measure of detachment, both from the emotion of others around him and from the crisis itself, observing it clinically, dispassionately. And he must focus his thinking strictly on the decisions he needs to make, rather than on the consequences that might follow if his decisions are wrong. This detachment and focus will afford him as much isolation as circumstances allow, and they will make him resistant to the emotional tumult around him. From there, the leader must draw upon his inner strength.

Every crisis must eventually come to an end. And even a leader who maintains her emotional balance throughout a crisis is likely to pay a price for doing so. Where previously she had reserves of strength, now she has a mass of unresolved tension built up during the course of the crisis. Left unresolved, the tension will make her first priority simply to avoid going through anything like that again. That sentiment is healthy to the extent the crisis should have been avoided in the first place. But crises are a part of leadership, and a leader who seeks always to avoid them will distort her judgment in doing so. Hence the leader must release the tension; and that means she must find solitude.

Grant used solitude this way in May 1864, during the Battle of the Wilderness, when for the first time he led the Army of the Potomac against the forces of General Robert E. Lee. In many respects Grant's troops fared no better than Hooker's had the year before. But where Hooker sought emotional release through histrionics, Grant found his in solitude. And thus in the end, Grant emerged with his emotional balance intact.

EVEN A STOIC has his emotional limits. By all accounts, Ulysses S. Grant—who became general-in-chief of the United States Army in March 1864—was an undemonstrative leader. One observer wrote that Grant "confines himself to saying and doing as little as possible before his men." Another quipped that Grant was "a man who could be silent in several languages." Grant's military secretary, Adam Badeau, contrasted him with Sherman: "Grant was calmer in manner a hundred fold. The habitual expression on his face was so quiet as to be incomprehensible." The contrast extended to other generals as well. A Union soldier at Vicksburg wrote: "Here was no McClelland, begging the boys to allow him to light his cigar on theirs, or inquiring to what regiment that exceedingly fine-marching company belonged . . . There was no nonsense, no sentiment; only a plain business man of the republic, there for the one single purpose of getting that command over the river in the shortest time possible." Grant was no-nonsense in appearance too, typically wearing a common soldier's blouse, unbuttoned, and old cavalry pants stuffed into muddy boots. A doctor who served under Grant at Vicksburg wrote that he was "as plain as an old shoe," and that when new recruits saw him, they were incredulous that he was their commander. Sometimes the results were comic. Once, during a lull in the fighting at the Wilderness, Grant strolled down the dirt road from his headquarters as a cattle drover approached from the opposite direction with his herd. One of the cattle strayed toward Grant, prompting the drover to yell: "I say, stranger, head off that critter for me, will you?" Without changing his expression, the general-in-chief stepped forward, threw up his hands, and shouted to the animal, causing it to return to the herd. Then Grant continued on his stroll as if nothing had happened.

Yet beneath the common demeanor lay an uncommon intensity. Sherman wrote that Grant "remembered the most minute details and watched every point." An enlisted soldier said that Grant knew every regiment "and in fact every cannon. He will ride along the long line of the army, apparently an indifferent observer, yet he sees and notices everything." And his secretary, Badeau, wrote that "in battle, the sphinx awoke. The outward calm was even then not entirely broken; but the utterance was prompt, the ideas were rapid, the judgment was decisive, the words were those of command. The whole man became intense, as it were, with a white heat."

Grant displayed that intensity in solitude as well. One example came at Vicksburg, where for months Grant faced a serious problem that defied solution. Some thirty-five thousand Confederates occupied a fort on a high bluff above the Mississippi River, with powerful batteries trained on the water below. So long as the rebels held that position the river was cut in two, with northern shipping unable to reach New Orleans, which Union forces had held since early 1862. Grant's task, beginning in late 1862, was to seize the fort and thereby open the length of the river to shipping once again. By March 1863, with forty-seven thousand soldiers at his command, Grant had employed seven different schemes to do just that: digging canals, sending boats full of men across swamps and up bayous, anything he could do to get his men from the west side of the river (where they were then) to the east, from which they could attack the fort on dry land from the rear. Every one of the schemes had failed. At that point Grant appeared to be yet another unsuccessful Union commander, with growing calls in Washington and the press for his replacement.

But then Grant holed up in the former ladies' cabin of his head-quarters boat, the *Magnolia*, to devise a new plan entirely on his own. There, night after night, he spent long hours alone, sitting at his mahogany desk, "withdrawn behind a barrier of intense preoc-cupation" as he pored over maps and smoked cigar after cigar. Indeed, Grant's concentration was so total that he often retained his seated posture as he got up to retrieve a document or map from a nearby table. Throughout this time Grant shared his thoughts with no one. Finally, very late one night, one of his best lieuten-ants, James McPherson, confronted Grant in his smoke-filled room. "General, this won't do," McPherson said. "You are injuring yourself. Join us in a few toasts, and throw this burden off your mind." Grant looked up and said that whiskey was not the answer. If McPherson really wanted to help him, Grant said, he "could give him a dozen cigars and leave him alone."

When Grant was done, he came forth with a plan so radical that almost every one of his lieutenants implored him not to proceed with it. Union ironclads—armored naval vessels equipped with heavy cannon—had already tried to run past Vicksburg's batteries and been badly mauled as a result. Now Grant proposed to make the run again, this time at night—though Confederate sentries lined the shoreline, ready to torch great stacks of hay to light the river for the guns high above. And Grant would make the run with nearly every ironclad he had, accompanied by all of his transport ships, wooden vessels whose thin skins a cannonball would pass clean through. Meanwhile, on marshy ground to the west, Grant's troops would march forty miles south to New Carthage, where, according to the plan, they would board the transports, cross the river, and fight their way onto dry ground on the river's eastern shore. From there, Grant's army would wheel north, toward Vicksburg, operating without a line of supply and living off the land for food—two things that no army of that size had ever done before. And all the while, Grant would face an opposing army of unknown and perhaps equal size, which for its part would have the advantages of interior lines and a populace that informed them of Grant's every move.

Sherman, especially, saw "the whole thing as one of the most hazardous or desperate moves of this or any other war." Indeed, he regarded the idea as downright unmilitary, contradicting any number of axioms of war. Sherman wrote to his wife just before the ironclads shoved off on April 16: "I tremble at the result." The ironclads' commander, David Porter, was game for the effort but made clear its all-or-nothing stakes: once the gunboats went below the batteries, he told Grant, "we give up all hopes" of getting them back upstream.

But despite all the risks, and despite all the violations of rules laid down at West Point, Grant's plan was the most brilliant of any executed by either side during the war. Vicksburg fell to Union forces on July 4, cementing Grant's position, in Lincoln's mind above all, as the Union's foremost general. Grant's plan was a work of creative genius, which rejected the standards of his day when they hampered his purpose. In that respect Grant's creativity was just like T. E. Lawrence's fifty years later, when Lawrence rejected the standards of his day to develop the concept of insurgency. But though both men used solitude for a common purpose, the ways they did so were subtly different. Lawrence—like Jane Goodall yet another fifty years later—used solitude for intuition, as insights that had been percolating beneath his consciousness for months finally surfaced in the stillness of his tent. (Tents seem to help intuition—Goodall lived in one too.) Grant, in contrast, used solitude for hard analytical work, beginning with a general idea that he had consciously held for months—"I think our troops must get below the city to be used effectively"—and then working that idea into something specific (and more radical) as he studied the detail in his documents and maps. But the key to both men's creativity was the same: in solitude, each of them could see where conventional thinking obstructed their purposes, and then find ways around it.

THE FOLLOWING SPRING Grant used solitude during combat itself, this time to preserve his emotional balance. On May 4, 1864—now as general-in-chief of the entire federal army, but with his headquarters in the field with the Army of the Potomac, and thus as its de facto commander—Grant prepared to retrace a route that exactly one year before had led to Lee's greatest victory. In May 1863, Joseph Hooker, as commander of the same Army, had crossed the Rappahannock River near Chancellorsville, Virginia, to launch an attack in Lee's rear. "Fighting Joe" Hooker was many things Grant was not: blond, dashing, egotistical, and so prone to grandiose bluster that Lincoln wrote a letter chastising him about it only two days after Hooker assumed command. But all that bluster turned to smoke after he came into contact with Lee. Hooker's initial attack came as a shock to Lee's Army of Northern Virginia, whose soldiers at that moment were divided into two groups nearly sixteen miles apart. Yet Lee hung on until he could unite all his forces, and then Stonewall Jackson launched a surprise attack of his own, rolling up Hooker's right flank in what was arguably Lee's finest hour as a commander. Hooker was literally struck dumb by the chaos that followed, staring blankly as he stood next to a white pillar at the Chancellorsville mansion that served as his headquarters, with Confederate shells roaring past overhead, until finally his army beat an ignominious retreat to the north. The two armies would not collide again until Gettysburg, by which time Hooker was long gone as commander.

Now Grant marched toward the same enemy, on the same ground where Hooker had so completely lost his nerve the year before. Grant crossed the Rapidan River—a large tributary of the Rappahannock, which joined it near Chancellorsville—at noon on May 4, 1864. Like Hooker, Grant had never before met Lee in combat. Grant led approximately 110,000 men; Lee, 65,000. But upon crossing the Rapidan, Grant's army would need to march through the Wilderness, an area of extremely dense forest and undergrowth that Lee knew intimately. The dense forest would also impede Grant's ability to manage his troops in battle; so his intention was to march his men quickly through the Wilderness on May 4 and then seek to engage Lee on the more open ground beyond.

Yet those plans did not last the day. Grant's men marched southeast through the Wilderness, along the Germanna Ford Road. As his men reached the very center of the forest, however, they learned that rebel troops were approaching along the Orange Turnpike, which ran northeast toward the Germanna Ford Road, intersecting with it at Wilderness Tavern, a deserted, ramshackle structure that had seen its share of action the year before. (Stonewall Jackson's amputated arm was buried there.) Grant probably could have pushed on and gotten his troops past the Wilderness, but that would have left the long tail of his supply wagons exposed to destruction by the Confederates. So Grant halted his men to allow the wagons to catch up later that afternoon. Grant slept soundly that night, but many of his men did not, especially those who had fought on that ground the year before. In those dark woods they felt "a sense of ominous dread which many of [them] found it almost impossible to shake off"—a sense augmented by the frequent sight of skulls and "skeletons in rotted blue, washed partly out of their shallow graves by the rains of the past winter."

Grant thought that Lee would probably leave most of his men behind some old defenses—prepared, like the shallow graves, the year before—just west of the Wilderness. But at dawn the next morning, Grant's men were shocked to see the Confederate 2nd Corps, commanded by Dick Ewell, dug in for battle astride the Orange Turnpike, close to Grant's 5th Corps, commanded by Gouverneur K. Warren. Grant's reaction was aggressive, ordering that "if any opportunity presents itself for pitching into a part of Lee's army, do so without giving time for disposition." At ten A.M.

Grant rode to the front, where the situation was already unraveling. Another strong Confederate force—Lee's 3rd Corps, commanded by the pugnacious A. P. Hill—was approaching along the Orange Plank Road, which ran parallel to the Orange Turnpike. Warren's soldiers thus faced a nearly continuous Confederate line comprising more than two-thirds of Lee's troops. George Meade—the nominal chief of the Army of the Potomac, who now served loyally as Grant's second-in-command—was disconcerted because he had thought the rebels would merely try to delay the Union march, rather than start a battle in earnest. But that, by all appearances, was exactly what Lee was about to do. And two-thirds of Grant's men were not in position yet.

At that point "Grant calmly took charge," gently assuring Meade that if Lee wanted to fight in the Wilderness, "that is all right." Grant ordered his largest corps, the 2nd, commanded by Winfield Scott Hancock—whom Grant regarded as the best corps commander in the entire Union army, and who had been grievously wounded at Gettysburg while his men repulsed Pickett's Charge—to move up quickly and strike Hill's smaller force. Then Grant rode with Meade to a meadow a mile behind the lines, where his staff was already pitching tents for an impromptu headquarters. There "Grant took a seat on a convenient stump, lighted another of the twenty cigars he distributed among the various pockets of his uniform at the start of every day, and sat calmly, an imperturbable figure wreathed in tobacco smoke." Then—apart from the group, alone with his thoughts between the dispatches and decisions that followed—Grant took out his penknife, picked up a stick, and began whittling. By that simple device, Grant created some space to stay focused on his own thoughts as best he could.

By midafternoon Hancock was making gains. But then one of Grant's aides, Horace Porter, ran back to headquarters with sad news for Grant personally: his lifelong friend, Brigadier General Alexander Hays, had been shot in the head while leading his men forward. Porter wrote that "General Grant by no means was a demonstrative man, but he was visibly affected. He was seated upon the ground with his back against a tree, still whittling pine sticks." Gathering his thoughts—in solitude, despite those around him—Grant "sat for a time without uttering a word," and then managed to speak about his old friend only after pausing to gather himself after each sentence. Hancock nearly routed Hill later that day, but darkness fell before he could finish the job.

Grant's plan for May 6 was simple: reinforce Hancock with everything the army could spare and then crush Lee's right, which in turn might allow Grant to crush Lee's army altogether. In the early light the plan began to work; Hill's men retreated in a sort of controlled rout, and Hancock sent word back that "we are driving them most beautifully." But Lee had another corps on the way, commanded by his best general, James "Pete" Longstreet, who had marched his men thirty-two miles in twenty-four hours to reach the battlefield. For the Confederates, he arrived just in time. By then bullets were flying around Lee himself, who was rather conspicuously mounted on his white horse, Traveller, as he made a desperate last effort to rally his men. Normally an archetype of dignified reserve, Lee was "overcome with emotion" as he saw the fresh columns approach, rising high in his stirrups and waving his wide hat.

Longstreet's first action was to shoo Lee to the rear—Lee was "off his balance" with elation, Longstreet later recalled. That done, Longstreet arranged his Texans into a compact formation and drove them straight into Hancock's troops. By nine A.M., Hancock's men had retreated back to where they started; by ten, Union troops began streaming through Grant's headquarters, leaving his staff in turmoil.

But if others were losing their heads, Grant was not. He continued to give "his orders calmly and coherently," one witness said, "without any external sign of undue tension or agitation." Another observer confirmed the point, saying that Grant "never exhibited to better advantage his peculiar ability in moving troops with unparalleled speed to critical points on the line of battle, or, as it was sometimes called, 'feeding a fight.'" Then a handful of Confederate shells exploded nearby. Grant stood up, puffed on his cigar, surveyed the scene, and then sat back down on his stump. A staff officer suggested to him that they move their headquarters farther to the rear. Without moving from his seat, Grant stopped whittling for a moment, eyeballed the man, and quietly said: "It strikes me that it would be better to order up some artillery and defend the present location." Then he started whittling again.

But soon Grant had a real crisis on his hands, and then two of them. The disorder of Hancock's retreat had left his left flank "in the air," meaning open to attack, just as Hooker's right flank had been in the air at Chancellorsville—in that case with campaign-ending results. Longstreet soon spotted the exposed flank and sent five thousand men forward to roll it up. The result was panic on the Union left; "our lines broke and ran like sheep," a Union soldier wrote in his diary. Then Longstreet drove the rest of his men forward in a frontal attack, causing two of Hancock's four divisions to scatter. Now the Union army was in danger of disintegrating. But in the chaos that followed, Longstreet himself was accidentally shot by his own men—just as Stonewall Jackson had been shot by his own men after his flank attack the year before, just four miles away. (Longstreet survived; Jackson did not.) That allowed Hancock frantically to re-form his lines, just before Lee hit him with everything he could, in a smaller-scale reprise of Pickett's effort the year before. The result this time was the same: Hancock held the line.

Then Grant faced an even graver crisis. It turned out that his flank at the opposite end of the battlefield was "in the air" too, just as Hancock's had been after his retreat. Grant's general up there was the usually solid John Sedgwick, who commanded the 6th Corps, which was dug in near where Grant had crossed the Rapidan. Lee's general at that end, Ewell, had been too timid to exploit the vulnerability, but Lee heard about it late that afternoon and immediately ordered an attack. At six P.M. his men hit Sedgwick's flank end-on, rolling it up more than a mile and cutting off Grant's access to the Rapidan. An hour later two flustered staffers came riding in from that quarter to report to headquarters that all was lost on the Union right. Meade exploded at them, and they galloped away. Then a brigadier general rode in from that same direction and delivered a similar message. "This is a crisis that cannot be looked upon too seriously," he declared to Grant. "I know Lee's methods well by past experience. He will throw his whole army between us and the Rapidan, and cut us off from our communications." This time it was Grant's turn finally to lose his patience. He got up from his stump, removed his cigar from his mouth, and turned on the man. "Oh, I am heartily tired of hearing about what *Lee* is going to do," he said. "Some of you always seem to think he is suddenly going to turn a double somersault and land in our rear and on both our flanks at the same time. Go back to your command and try to think what we are going to do ourselves, instead of what *Lee* is going to do."

Yet still more reports of disaster streamed in from that quarter. John Rawlins, Grant's chief of staff—and in some things Grant's personal guardian—told a friend hours later that "the coming of officer after officer with additional details soon made it apparent that the general was confronted with the greatest crisis of his life." Finally, after nightfall, the word came that Sedgwick had re-formed and held his line. For the time being, at least, Grant's army was safe.

Only then—after his flanks were secured, and the fighting done for the day—did Grant reveal the strain he had been under. The revelation came in an act of deliberate solitude, different in kind from his solitude at Vicksburg but just as intense. A year before, Hooker had broken on the inside, and thereby had broken altogether. For the past two days, Grant had faced even greater dangers than Hooker did—Grant's losses totaled 17,666, more than Hooker's, and Grant had both of his flanks rolled up, rather than just one. Whittling on his stump, Grant had borne those strains, and the loss of his lifelong friend Hays, "without uttering any word of doubt or discouragement." Now, with the danger past, Grant allowed himself to break on the outside; and even then, as Shelby Foote points out, Grant did so "with a degree of circumspection and detachment highly characteristic of the man." Only Rawlins and another trusted officer, Charles Francis Adams Jr. (grandson of the sixth president and great-grandson of the second) were there to witness it. "When all proper measures had been taken," Rawlins said, "Grant went into his tent, threw himself face downward on his cot, and gave way to the greatest emotion." Rawlins said that he had "never before seen him so deeply moved" and that "nothing could be more certain than that he was stirred to the depths of his soul." Adams was more succinct: "I never saw a man more agitated in my life."

Grant knew his emotional limits, and that he had passed them during his desperate first battle with Lee. Not that he had passed them in a sense of self-control; to the contrary, everything about his release—its timing, and the careful manner in which he executed it—showed that he retained his self-control throughout. Just like Lincoln after he heard about Lee's escape the summer before, Grant knew that the turmoil inside him was a threat to his continued effectiveness as a leader. (Lincoln wept from grief, Grant to release tension.) And Grant knew the turmoil would find an outlet somewhere—if not in a tent, then in a decision affecting his whole army. The most likely decision, if history was any guide, would be the same decision made by every one of his predecessors who had fought Lee in Virginia, namely to relieve the unbearable pressure in an altogether different way—by returning north. But Grant's solitude kept him pointed in the opposite direction.

Grant's solitude affected his men too. Late that night Grant sat by a campfire alone, long after everyone else at headquarters had gone to bed. In one tent, Sylvanus Cadwallader, a reporter whom Grant had taken into his inner circle, was unable to sleep. Cadwallader's faith in the army's course was deeply shaken by the events of the past two days. "Unpleasant thoughts ran riot through my mind," he later wrote. "We had waged two days of murderous battle, and had but little to show for it. Judged by comparative losses, it had been disastrous to the Union cause. We had been compelled by Gen. Lee to fight him on a ground of his own choos-ing, with the certainty of losing at least two men to his one . . . We had scarcely gained a rod of the battlefield at the close of a two days' contest." And Cadwallader's faith in Grant himself was shaken. "For minutes that seemed hours, for the first and only time, during my intimate and confidential relations with Gen. Grant, I began to question the grounds of my faith in him, so long entertained, and so unqualifiedly expressed. Could it be that I had followed Gen. Grant through the Tallahatchie expedition; the operations against Vicksburg; the campaign at Chattanooga; and finally to the dark and tangled thickets of the Wilderness; to record his defeat and overthrow, as had been recorded of every commander of the Army of the Potomac?"

Finally Cadwallader got up and stepped outside his tent. "I happened to look obliquely to the right, and there sat Gen. Grant in an army chair on the other side of the slowly dying embers. His hat was drawn down over his face, the high collar of an old blue army overcoat turned up above his ears, one leg crossed over the other knee, eyes on the ashes in front, causing me to think him half asleep." But Grant spotted Cadwallader, straightened up in his chair, and "commenced a pleasant chatty conversation upon indifferent subjects." For the next half hour, neither man mentioned the events of the past two days. Finally, Cadwallader said that it was time for both of them to get some sleep, and "that it was a duty" in Grant's case "to get all the rest he could." Grant "smilingly assented," stood up, and spoke lightly of the "sharp work Gen. Lee had been giving us for a couple of days." Then he stepped into his tent.

Only then did Cadwallader realize that Grant had not shared his gloom in the least; all of it had poured out in Grant's tent. "It was the grandest mental sunburst of my life," Cadwallader wrote.

The next day Grant's men had a sunburst of their own, as they prepared for the inevitable march north—but instead were ordered south. Grant's restoration in solitude now became a restoration for the men he led. As exhausted as they were, the men cheered and threw their caps and crowded around him as he passed through their ranks on horseback. "Our spirits rose," one recalled later. "We marched free. The men began to sing . . . That night we were happy."

CHAPTER 9

Magnanimity
Aung San Suu Kyi, 1990

"Isolation is not something to be frightened of."
—AUNG SAN SUU KYI, IN *Voice of Hope*

Anger can distort a leader's judgment as much as fear can. Indeed for leaders, as for anyone else, fear converts into anger quite easily. The stress and strain of leadership—the fear that one is nearly, if not actually, overmatched by one's responsibilities—are emotional tinder for the leader who encounters adversity he does not expect. The adversity might give rise to a spark of irritation, as for a leader whose subordinates sometimes make the same mistake twice, or fail to anticipate something the leader is rather obviously going to need, or are careless in a way that adds to the leader's burdens unnecessarily. Or the adversity might bring a fire of its own, as when some crisis erupts unexpectedly or the leader personally is subjected to serious injustice. Leadership, like fertilizer, contains elements that can be volatile or nurturing, depending on how one handles them. An unreflective leader is prone to volatility: he does not realize that his own anxieties are part of the fuel for his anger about some external event, and thus his response—berating employees, torching a meeting—is disproportionate to the event itself. A leader of this type finds himself apologizing frequently if he is decent, or embittering his followers if he is not.

A more reflective leader can see these same events in a more constructive way. She will pause before reacting to adversity, because she knows she might overreact if she does not. And she will reflect on what caused the adversity in the first place. Subordinates make mistakes like everyone else, and in her day the leader might have made mistakes that were even worse. Rather than lash out whenever she has the chance, she will forgive the trespasses of others, as others have forgiven hers. And she will help her followers to learn from their mistakes—by describing the mistakes clearly and matter-of-factly, by explaining how to avoid them in the future, and then, if the occasion allows, by reassuring the person that the leader herself has made that kind of mistake too. Such is the difference between leading one's followers and scalding them while blowing off steam.

Reflection can also help the leader manage her response to injustice directed at her personally. Political-operator types might scheme to get ahead of her for a promotion; empire-builders might seek to arrogate power that is rightfully hers; a colleague to whom she was generous when that person was vulnerable might, when the tables are turned, treat her with spite. The leader might or might not need to defend herself against such actions, but how she reacts to them emotionally is another matter. Rather than let such actions upset her own emotional balance, she can reflect on the reasons that drove the person to them—fear, narcissism, or simply that the person is miserable in general. And having reflected on those reasons, the leader will take the action less personally, because those reasons are usually not about her. Indeed, she will often feel a degree of sympathy for the person: people who are miserable often have reasons to be, though perhaps they could have handled them better. Where otherwise one might feel anger, reflection helps to bring peace.

Aung San Suu Kyi suffered great personal injustice as a result of her efforts to bring democracy to Burma. Through meditation and reflection, however, she found magnanimity—and thereby preserved her ability to lead her cause to success.

FOR AUNG SAN Suu Kyi, solitude has often come not by choice. For more than fifteen years—from 1989 to 1995, from 2000 to

2002, and again from 2003 to 2010—she endured the forced isolation of house arrest, cut off from contact with her family and, with
limited exceptions, from the outside world. Yet her reaction was
more sublime than angry. After her first house arrest, she said, "I
feel spiritually stronger; in a sense I've been tested and that has
strengthened me. And I think I've learned to put a much greater
value on compassion. I think compassion is very important in this
world." Just how important, Suu Kyi would make clear by 2015.

Suu Kyi is the daughter of Aung San, who is to Burmese what
George Washington is to Americans, albeit more tragically. In
March 1945, when he was only thirty, Aung San commanded the
Patriot Burmese Forces, who fought alongside the Allies to liberate
Burma from the Japanese. In early 1947, Aung San negotiated
Burma's independence from Great Britain. His political party won
248 of 255 seats in elections held in April 1947, making him the
country's de facto leader. Only three months later, however—when
Suu Kyi was two years old—five gunmen (sent by a political opponent) murdered Aung San and most of his cabinet as they sat
around a conference table. In the decades that followed, the country devolved into totalitarian rule, led by General Ne Win, head of
the Burmese Army. In 1960, Ne Win sent Suu Kyi's mother, Khin
Kyi, to New Dehli as Burma's ambassador to India—as a way to
get her out of the country. Suu Kyi, then age fifteen, accompanied
her. Later, Suu Kyi attended Oxford; in 1972, she married Michael
Aris, an English scholar specializing in Tibetan culture. They
settled in Oxford, living quietly with their two young boys,
Alexander and Kim.

But a phone call one night in March 1988 changed all that. A
family friend in Burma called to say that Suu Kyi's mother had
suffered a stroke and was in critical condition in a hospital in
Rangoon. Michael later wrote, "She put down the phone and at
once started to pack. I had a premonition that our lives would
change for ever."

The next day Suu Kyi flew to Burma. She was still there, nursing
her mother in their family home in Rangoon, when in July 1988
the dictator Ne Win announced that he was relinquishing power,

effective immediately. The country was electrified, but within days another general, Sein Lwin, known as "the Butcher," assumed power. Mass demonstrations ensued. At first Suu Kyi played no public role in the protests, despite requests that she do so as the daughter of the country's most revered leader. But on August 26, in front of nearly a million people in Rangoon, she stepped forth to deliver a broadside in favor of multiparty elections. In fluent Burmese, she told the crowd: "I could not as my father's daughter remain indifferent to all that was going on. This national crisis could in fact be called the second struggle for national independence." Immediately Suu Kyi was regarded as the leader of the pro-democracy movement, and she began campaigning throughout the country.

On September 18, a new ruling junta, the State Law and Order Restoration Council—SLORC, as they were usually called, or the Council, as they will be called here—took power. The Council imposed martial law the same day. Over the next four days the army repeatedly opened fire upon the demonstrators, killing thousands. Yet the Council also announced that they would conduct "free and fair" elections at some later date. Later that month, Suu Kyi and two colleagues founded a new political party, the National League for Democracy, or NLD.

Suu Kyi's mother died on December 27, 1988. In the months that followed, Suu Kyi toured almost the entire country, speaking to enthusiastic crowds and consolidating her party's strength. But on July 20, 1989, at the Council's direction, Suu Kyi was arrested and ordered confined to her home for at least a year. More than forty of Suu Kyi's NLD colleagues were also arrested that day and sent to Insein Jail, which was notorious for its squalid conditions.

With the NLD's leadership confined or locked up, the Council proceeded with plans for elections the following spring. But the generals seriously misjudged the country's mood: on May 27, 1990, in elections that were by all accounts free and fair, the NLD swept 392 of 485 seats. Yet the Council effectively ignored the results, explaining after the fact that the elections were to choose a constitutional convention rather than a national assembly. The convention was never held.

Meanwhile, Suu Kyi began to adjust to what turned out to be almost six years of house arrest. "The first years were the worst," she recalled later. "They threw me in at the deep end." At first she received letters and parcels of food and books from her family; but when the Council released photographs of the parcels' contents shortly before the elections—as proof of its lenient treatment of her—she refused to receive the parcels or letters any longer. She also lacked telephone service, leaving her cut off from her husband and sons. Her roof leaked continuously—she moved buckets around to catch the water—and she refused to accept food from the government. Instead she exchanged her furniture, a bathtub, and her air-conditioning unit for money from the soldiers, but even then she could not afford enough food to sustain herself. (The military kept all of the "sold" items in a warehouse to return to her later.) Her weight dropped from 106 pounds to 90, her hair began to fall out, her eyesight dimmed, and she suffered heart problems. Yet Suu Kyi was kind to the individual soldiers who guarded her, asking about their families and making jokes. Throughout her confinement, the Council made clear that Suu Kyi was free to rejoin her family in England whenever she wished—in which case they would not allow her to return to Burma. She was never tempted by the offer.

Although Suu Kyi grew weaker physically, she kept herself strong mentally. Sometimes late at night, she would wake up, walk downstairs, and look at her father's photograph on the wall. "I would say to him then, 'It's you and me, Father, against them,' and I felt very comforted by his presence. I felt at times as if he was there with me." Each morning she arose at four thirty and engaged in an hour of *vipassana* meditation, a Buddhist technique in which mental concentration is focused upon conscious breathing. Then she listened to foreign broadcasts on her short-wave radio—her only contact with the outside world—before exercise and then breakfast. The rest of the day she devoted to study, playing piano (Bach helped keep her mind sharp), and household chores.

Of these activities, the centerpiece was Suu Kyi's meditation. The practice was new to her. Shortly before her house arrest, Suu Kyi had visited U Pandita, a renowned teacher of Buddhist meditation in Rangoon and the author of the seminal book *In This Very Life*. Michael sent the book to Suu Kyi early in her house arrest. "I remember everything he has taught me," Suu Kyi says of U Pandita. For U Pandita, meditation is a process to purify not only the practitioner, but society as a whole. At the core of this idea is the Buddhist concept of *metta*, or "loving-kindness." "In contrast to the aggressive, destructive quality of hatred," U Pandita writes, "*metta* wishes the welfare and happiness of others." "Engaged Buddhism is active compassion or active *metta*," Suu Kyi says. "It means not just sitting there passively saying, 'I feel sorry for them.' It means doing something about the situation by bringing whatever relief you can to those who need it most, by caring for them, by doing what you can to help others." A closely related concept is *karunna*, or "active compassion." Together, these concepts allow one not to hate one's oppressors but instead to feel sympathy for them, by cultivating an awareness of the forces—notably fear— that cause them to act as they do.

Through her meditation practice each morning, Suu Kyi overcame any sense of anger in response to the hardships of her captivity. By cultivating *metta* and *karunna* as her core values, Suu Kyi was able to view her captors with what she called "a breadth of vision," and thus to forgive them. "To forgive, I think, basically means the ability to see the person apart from the deed and to recognize that although he has done that deed, it does not mean he is irredeemable. There are aspects of him that are acceptable." Thus, for Suu Kyi, *metta* led to magnanimity. Indeed, with irony that was likely intended, Suu Kyi expressed a measure of gratitude for her time alone. "A lot of us within the organization have been given the opportunity to develop spiritual strength because we have been forced to spend long years by ourselves under detention and in prison. In a way, we owe it to the people who put us there."

Suu Kyi was released from house arrest on July 10, 1995. By then, *metta* had become the foundation of her philosophy of nonviolent resistance to the Burmese regime. When Suu Kyi's father, Aung San, was voted into power in 1947, he had said he would govern "on the basis of loving kindness and truth." Now Suu Kyi was prepared to emulate him. What she now advocated, she said, was a "revolution of the spirit . . . a political system which is guided by certain spiritual values." In a May 1996 speech, she asked the audience to identify the founding principle of the democratic movement in Burma, and herself answered:

> It is *metta*. Rest assured that if we should lose this *metta*, the whole democratic party would disintegrate. *Metta* is not only to be applied to those that are connected with you. It should also be applied to those who are against you. *Metta* means sympathy for others . . . We are an organization that is free from grudge and puts *metta* to the fore.

Suu Kyi's pledge to be "free from grudge" was put to even more severe tests in the years ahead. In January 1999, her husband, Michael, was diagnosed with prostate cancer. He had less than three months to live, but the Burmese regime refused to allow him to enter the country to visit Suu Kyi for a final time. Michael died on March 27, 1999, his fifty-third birthday. In September of the following year, after a nine-day standoff between Suu Kyi and Army troops who refused to let her travel beyond the city limits of Rangoon, the regime again placed Suu Kyi under house arrest. She was released more than a year and a half later, on May 27, 2002. Almost exactly a year later, on May 30, 2003, when traveling through the countryside (near Depayin) with about a hundred friends and supporters, Suu Kyi's caravan was attacked by regime-sponsored thugs whose goal was to kill her. They failed in that goal but killed seventy of her followers. After the attack, Suu Kyi was first taken to the Insein Jail, ostensibly for her own safety. Three months later she was placed under house arrest, now for the third time.

Yet Suu Kyi's commitment to *metta* and *karunna* remained unshaken. Only days after the Depayin massacre, Suu Kyi told a

UN envoy that she was willing to "turn the page." The prime minister at the time, Khin Nyunt—who had no involvement in the Depayin attack—began secret negotiations with Suu Kyi for a comprehensive political settlement. An agreement was drafted in May 2004, but another member of the ruling junta—Than Shwe, the man who had ordered the Depayin massacre—rejected it. "We were almost there," Suu Kyi later said.

Suu Kyi remained confined to her home throughout 2005 and into September 2006, when Burma's monks took to the streets. The monks are a powerful moral force in Burma, much like the Catholic Church is in countries that are predominantly Catholic. The month before, the regime had abruptly ended fuel subsidies, sending transportation costs soaring. Sporadic protests broke out, which the government violently suppressed. Then the monks began a "peace march" through Rangoon, walking barefoot in their saffron-colored robes, their numbers swelling to perhaps a hundred thousand, their columns stretching nearly a mile. Over and over they chanted the Metta Sutta, which begins, "May all sentient beings be cheerful and endowed with a happy life." On October 24, a column of monks passed through barricades and marched toward the gate of Suu Kyi's home, where she stood watching them with tears in her eyes. The monks' gesture was a moral endorsement of her leadership. Suu Kyi's embrace of *metta* thus came full circle: just as Suu Kyi had honored the monks' teachings through her practice of meditation, now they honored her.

Yet Suu Kyi's house arrest would continue for another four years, until she was finally released on November 13, 2010. By then she had spent more than fifteen of the previous twenty-one years confined to her home. Through meditation, Suu Kyi had made *metta* and *karunna* her spiritual core, and by doing so she maintained a sublime emotional balance throughout. And by making these values her political core as well, Suu Kyi presented herself to the regime not as an implacable foe, but as someone with whom a more enlightened leader could reach an accommodation.

In 2011, such a leader finally appeared. Thein Sein, inaugurated as president that year, promptly invited Suu Kyi to attend an economic conference and then to have dinner with him and his wife. Thein Sein was a genuine reformer who sought better relations with the West, and in that effort he did not see Suu Kyi "as a menace, a subversive or an agent of foreign powers" but rather as, "potentially at least, a vital ally." Soon Thein Sein began to implement reforms: trade unions were legalized, some political prisoners were released, and the NLD was permitted to register as a political party again. Thein Sein also suspended work on a controversial dam project because, he said, it was "against the will of the people"—an interest never before recognized by the regime. Eventually Thein Sein set November 8, 2015, as a date for nationwide elections in Burma. As in 1990, the elections were for the most part free and fair, and again the NLD won in a landslide, with Suu Kyi as the party's head. But this time, Thein Sein made clear, the election results would stand.

What Suu Kyi had found in isolation was not anger or fear, but "the real change that comes from inside, through learning the value of compassion, justice and love."

PART IV

CHAPTER 10
Moral Courage

Frank M. Johnson Jr. was probably the most consequential federal district court judge of the past sixty years. Tall, with chiseled features and an intimidating manner in court—one lawyer said that Johnson would peer over his reading glasses "looking at you like he's aiming down a rifle barrel"—Johnson did more than any other judge in the South to strike down the laws of Jim Crow. Johnson was appointed by President Dwight Eisenhower to the federal district bench in Montgomery, Alabama, on November 7, 1955. Over the next fifteen years, Johnson outlawed segregation on city buses and in Alabama's jails, prisons, and schools, enjoined the Ku Klux Klan from violence against Freedom Riders, and ordered the state to allow Martin Luther King and his followers to march from Selma to Montgomery. For all those actions, however, there were reactions: Johnson received death threats, white supremacists burned crosses on his yard, a Klansman blew up a dynamite bomb at the home of Johnson's mother (the Klansman thought Johnson himself lived there), and George Wallace made Johnson the principal target of his rhetoric during his successful 1962 campaign for governor. All the while, one Montgomery physician recalls about Johnson, "nobody took his defense. Not the newspapers. No ministers. No lawyers. Nobody defended him during those years." Johnson himself recalled, "There were many times I felt alone. I don't care who you are, when something happens and the entire state rises up, through its politicians and its press, and lambastes you and the Klan is making threats, you become apprehensive for your family, sometimes waiting for something to happen."

Yet Johnson never wavered from his duty. Virtually every judge spends time reflecting in chambers, and Johnson had strong values to reflect upon. Johnson grew up in rural northwestern Alabama, in Winston County—which had sent more soldiers to the Union Army than to the Confederate during the Civil War—and where, as Johnson put it, people "believe in a person's dignity, and they believe each person is possessed of and is entitled to integrity. They believe that without regard to race, creed, color, or ideology." Later, Johnson served in General George Patton's 3rd Army as an infantry officer in Normandy, where he was wounded twice. As a judge, Johnson picked up where he had left off as a soldier: one of his law clerks said that Johnson's actions were "always measured by what was the right thing to do for the United States." And Johnson had clear ideas about his judicial role: a judge's "sole duty," he said, "is to ascertain what the law is and make application of that law to the facts presented in any particular case. This is as far as his authority goes, and it should be as far as his concern goes." Against these core principles, the rants of George Wallace or the snubs of Johnson's neighbors would make no headway.

SOME LEADERSHIP DECISIONS bring consequences that are more than professional. Frequently those consequences take the form of moral criticism, where opponents criticize not only the decision itself, but the person who would dare make it. During the 1930s, for example, Churchill was derided as a warmonger because he advocated increased military spending to counter the Nazi threat. Dissenters from other forms of conventional wisdom—which today often take the form of absolutes, not least on college campuses—can expect similar treatment. And a dissenter from the orthodoxy of one's own tribe—be it a political party or any group that finds itself in competition with other groups—faces charges of betrayal. Even small decisions can bring moral criticism: the leader who closes her door to think is aloof; so is the leader who skips boondoggle conventions in favor of getting actual work done; so is the leader who spends time with family rather than at after-work gatherings for drinks; and the leader who answers some e-mails slowly, and others not at all, is derelict. All of these decisions involve nonconformity with the assumptions, and sometimes the cherished premises, of persons who do conform. And conformists often have a large investment, materially or psychologically, in those premises. Hence the nonconformist can expect some measure of invective in response.

Other decisions by their nature affect the leader personally. Sometimes the consequences are material, as with a decision to leave a lucrative job for a more fulfilling but less lucrative one. Other consequences weigh upon one's conscience, as with a decision that imposes hardship on some people in order to alleviate it for others. Still other times a leader faces material and psychological consequences alike, as an entrepreneur does when she leaves the security of an established organization to take the risk of starting her own. And beyond those consequences the leader can again expect moral criticism—that she is selfish, irresponsible, or callous.

The very point of these criticisms is to enforce conformity, and thus to prevent the leader from making these decisions in the first place. Moral courage is what enables a leader to make them nonetheless. It requires not only clarity, but conviction. And to have conviction, and thus moral courage, the leader must get her soul involved.

FIRST PRINCIPLES ARE a deep vein of moral courage. "Leaders who are well anchored in what they believe are going to be more effective," says Doug Conant, formerly president and CEO of the Campbell Soup Company, and a leader widely admired for his focus on integrity and results. Conant also served as president of the Nabisco Foods Company and is the founder and CEO of ConantLeadership and the coauthor of the bestselling *TouchPoints: Creating Powerful Leadership Connections in the Smallest of Moments.* "Leaders need to work on personal leadership as well as organizational leadership," he says. "Leadership is an inside-out process. You need to be fortified within before you can lead the people around you."

Like General Mattis, Conant worries that leaders today do not reflect enough. "I'm astounded by the lack of introspection among leaders," Conant says. "It's not that you need to be completely unplugged from the outside world. But you do need to be completely plugged in to what *you* think. Shakespeare said, 'To thine own self be true.' But you can't be true to yourself if you don't know yourself in a deeper way. And you can't know yourself without introspection." Conant himself struggled on this point early in his career. "For my first ten years, when I was at General Mills, I worried about making others happy, rather than about what I thought was important. Then I was let go."

Since then Conant has made a dedicated practice of reflecting on his first principles. "Every morning, for thirty minutes, I sit in the garden or in a comfortable chair with a cup of coffee, reflecting," he says. "I think about five things: my family, my work, my community, my faith, and my personal well-being. I think about how I'm doing with each of these things, what's working, what isn't, what I need to change." Every three or four months, Conant does what he calls a "deeper dive." "It's usually when I'm traveling, on a plane or train coming home. I'll go through each of these five things, and get reconnected with my values and my different roles in life. It's a wonderful way of keeping me centered on what I truly believe." Once a year, Conant also revises what he calls his "Personal Mission Statement." "For years, I would go to Utah for a few days alone, and give myself the gift of time to reflect on what I've accomplished and what I want to focus on in the coming year." Conant says that his process of daily, seasonal, and annual reflection is "a discipline I've stuck with for twenty-five to thirty years. It makes me more authentic with other people, and more effective, because my thinking is pretty fresh on what matters most to me. Introspection helps ensure that my decisions are aligned with my principles. It's life-changing. And the only person equipped to have this conversation with yourself is you."

Conant stresses the need for a leader to reflect on first principles before adversity strikes. "As a leader, you need to have a rudder in the water for the storms of life. You'll have smooth sailing at times, but you know the storms will come. You need to be prepared for that."

Conant describes an instance where his reflection on first principles gave him the moral courage to "defy the critics," as he puts it. "I was recruited to join RJR Nabisco three years after the leveraged buyout that was the subject of the book *Barbarians at the Gate*." While there, Conant was assigned the position of senior vice president of marketing for Nabisco Biscuit Company, then a $5.5 billion operation. "It was the most dysfunctional environment I'd ever gone into," he says. "Everyone felt like a victim, and the mindset seemed to be that the ends justified the means. They were clearly talented people who had lost their way a bit. I ordered a survey of employee attitudes from a veteran consultant who had conducted thousands of these surveys. He said that our culture was 'swamp water.' Our employees had the lowest levels of trust he had ever seen." Yet Conant refused to conform to a prevailing norm that he thought unacceptable. "One of my core beliefs is that we can't expect an employee to value the organization until we've tangibly shown that the organization values the employee." So Conant began to take steps to recognize employees who had shown initiative in improving the company's culture. "I didn't get a lot of encouragement at first. Skeptics said my approach was 'soft' or 'lovey-dovey.'" But Conant held firm, disregarded the critics, and moved forward with his overall plan. A year later he commissioned another survey of employee attitudes. "The same consultant told me, 'This is unbelievable. You've gone from swamp water to Perrier!'

"I never could have gotten through that leadership challenge if I hadn't been anchored by my process of reflection," Conant says. "The time for introspection is before you need it."

DENA BRAEGER ECHOES Conant's point about awareness of one's first principles, or what she calls "priorities." "People are so quick to bow to the idea of 'staying connected,'" she says. "They aren't conscious of the priorities they're setting with regard to their

time. Time is an unrenewable resource. You can't get it back. All
these things we've done to exchange information, to access information at our fingertips, have actually taken away our time for
restoring the soul. You're giving away your soul's ability to be
moved. If we'd spend more time in solitude, we'd value ourselves
more."

Dena has ample courage to disregard the norm of constant
connectivity. "Solitude is soul-restorative. In solitude, I realize
again what's most important to me. I can hear my own voice again.
Afterward, when I face choices, I know who I am, what my choices
will be. I won't be afraid to make them."

DAN BROSTEK'S EXPERIENCE illustrates Conant's point about
finding moral courage through reflection on first principles. Like
many people, Dan reflects most deeply during long runs. "I run to
understand who I am, what's meaningful to me," he says. Dan
grew up in a military family in upstate New York, graduated from
West Point in 1996, and then joined Aetna as an executive after
leaving the military. "I had a good twelve-year run there," Dan
says. "It was good financially, I was promoted numerous times,
and I grew a lot in terms of professional development." Then Dan
moved to an executive position at Merkle, an agency that provides
marketing services for large insurance companies. "At Merkle
I was working with our clients' marketing officers to provide their
departments with a variety of media and data-management
services. The people at Merkle were very impressive. And I understood the clients, especially in the health-care area, because I had
worked in their industry myself." Although Dan's success continued at Merkle, a sense of fulfillment did not come with it. "Things
looked good on the outside, but on the inside I felt an emptiness.
I had this nagging sense that my work was not meaningful to me,
that something bigger was calling." Dan is married with two
young sons, and at one point he asked his boys if they knew what
he did for a living. "You work on the computer all day," one said.
"You work for eBay," said the other. "At that point," Dan says, "I
realized that my kids had no idea who I work for, or what I do."

Dan began thinking about these concerns during his runs. He had become an avid runner a few years after leaving the military. "I had gone from being in the best shape of my life to the worst. The trigger moment came during an annual trip to Hilton Head with three of my West Point buddies who were still in the military. They were all in great shape; I looked like a pasty-white beached whale. I had gotten sucked into the corporate grind, and with it went my physical health." Dan trained for and ran in the Hartford Marathon and then got into trail running. "I knew immediately that trail running was different for me than road running. Trail running puts you in nature, which is a meaningful place," Dan says. "You trade the stimulation of an urban environment for sublimity. That encourages deeper and uninterrupted thinking about what's meaningful." Another difference is specific to Dan. "I'm a very analytical person. My mind is constantly grinding away. I can't break that cycle when I'm running on a road, because I don't have to think about the act of running itself. So my mind just keeps cycling." But on the uneven ground of a trail, the cycle breaks. "For the first forty-five minutes, I'm focused on body place-ment, where each foot is landing on the trail. I'm in a monitoring mode. Then my body starts to gain muscle memory about where it's at on the trail." At that point—with the analytical cycle broken, and his body guiding itself along the trail—Dan's mind switches into what he calls "awareness." "My mind reboots," he says. The clarity is like that upon awakening after a good night's sleep. "I have this awareness of what's important in my life, and how I'm doing with those things."

Dan uses those periods of awareness to think about several of the things that Doug Conant thinks about—work, family, community. "I remember a conversation I had with my battalion commander before I was getting ready to leave the Army. He told me, 'As long as you can go to bed each night and lay your head on the pillow feeling like you did something meaningful, that's all that matters.' That really stuck with me. Later, when I was running, I realized that the things I was working toward each day—stock options, long-term compensation—weren't meaningful to me. I also

realized that I wasn't shaping my kids' lives the way I wanted to."
Around this time, Dan lost his mom after a long battle with cancer.
"She was sixty-five. I went for a run later that day and thought, 'If I
die at sixty-five, or fifty-five, will I have done everything I wanted
to do in life, everything I should do?' For me, those thoughts can
only come up on runs."

Dan also began connecting with parts of himself that were hard to
reach. "I'm a systems engineer by training. I take complicated problems, a difficult scenario, and think through solutions to them. But
I could never tap into the emotional side of myself. After my mom
died, I began to connect with those feelings on the trail." What Dan
began to bring forth was the raw materials of conviction. "I began to
fuse analytical clarity with my underlying raw feelings. I made a
connection between my analytical side and my emotional side."

For some time, Dan and his wife, Carrie, had thought about the
idea of moving out West. Now they began talking about that idea
more seriously. After a lot of discussion and working out the
numbers, they reached a decision: Dan would quit his job at
Merkle, and the family would move to Bend, Oregon, where he
would become director of marketing for a nonprofit. "It all began
to make sense for me," he says. "My work would be more fulfilling,
my family was excited to live out West, and I'd be contributing to
the community in an important way." His job would pay a fraction
of what his Merkle job did, but Dan was willing to make that
trade. "Once I expanded my decision-making criteria beyond
compensation, the decision was easy. We'd make some sacrifices
and pursue simplicity."

Dan recalls telling one of his clients at Merkle about the news.
"His first reaction was, 'Man, you're killing me, you just put a
team together for us.' As Dan told him more about the details,
however, his client said, 'Tell me more. I don't hear stories like
this.'" The client was wistful when Dan was done. "I've got the
handcuffs on me," the man said. "I'm going to purgatory."

THE IMPORTANCE OF solitude is one of Brené Brown's first principles as a leader. Brené is the author of three *New York Times*

number-one bestselling books (*Rising Strong*, *Daring Greatly*, and *The Gifts of Imperfection*) and a research professor at the University of Houston Graduate School of Social Work, where she studies "vulnerability, courage, worthiness, and shame." She is also the founder and CEO of the Daring Way and CourageWorks, which teaches individuals and organizations about bravery in leadership. "The biggest mistake I've made in my career to date is believing that solitude is a luxury," she says. "I could chart the ups and down of my quality of life personally and professionally and the amount of time I spend in solitude. It's a discipline that can make or break my work." For her, solitude takes a variety of forms. "It's a span of practices, long periods and short periods. I need both. On international flights, I don't sit next to anyone I'm traveling with. That gives me twelve hours of time to come up with ideas." Closer to home, she blocks out time on her calendar to think and write. "It's nonnegotiable." She also finds solitude while swimming. "No one can talk to you then."

Like many people, Brené has faced social pressure not to engage in solitude. "The decision to engage in solitude is a vulnerable and courageous act. There's a perception that making time for solitude is a sign of self-indulgence or weakness. Or people make smart-ass comments about it, like 'Are you going to meet the Dalai Lama?'" From her research, she sees that the pressure can be acute for new leaders. "When you ask them, 'What kind of alone time do you need to think through problems?' they'll say, 'I haven't earned that yet.' They think that only established leaders can do that. It goes back to the idea that solitude is self-indulgent." What these newer leaders don't realize, Brené says, is that "solitude is not the reward for great leadership. It's the path to great leadership."

Brené describes an instance when her belief in the importance of solitude gave her the courage to insist on it. "Just a few weeks ago I was working on building a new business with a very small, lean team. We were working seven days a week, meeting for ten hours a day. The company's president called me one night and said, 'Something's wrong. These meetings are starting to feel punitive. People are exhausted, angry.' I said, 'I know. I'm exhausted and

frustrated too.'" Although the group had another ten-hour meeting scheduled for the next day and several "deliverables" due a few
days later, Brené made a decision. "I said, 'I'm not coming in
tomorrow morning. I need to be alone.' The next day I swam,
walked three miles, and reorganized my pantry while in the house
alone." Then she went into the office around three P.M. "I said, 'Let
me start by apologizing. I've been micromanaging everyone here.
I'm exhausted because I can't do everything I feel I need to.
Everyone's exhausted. We need to stop for a while.' A couple of
people said, 'We've got X and Y that we need to get done.' I said,
'No one's working over the weekend. We're losing our humanity.'"
The group met again the following Monday morning. "We had
total clarity. In three hours, we got a ton done.

"To me, leadership means choosing courage over comfort,"
Brené says. "Part of that means choosing solitude over busyness."

"I'VE REALLY THOUGHT about what it is about solitude that
makes it so important for me as a leader," says Jimmy Bartz,
founder of Thad's, an Episcopal church in Los Angeles. "It's about
courage. I get the courage piece from solitude." Thad's (the name
comes from the apostle Thaddeus) is unconventional in its
approach. "The traditional approach to expanding the Church's
reach is to bring people into our space, to our way of doing things,"
Jimmy says. "At Thad's we turn ourselves out into the community.
We've operated out of buildings for a jazz club, the Jewish
Community Center, and a screenwriters' workshop. We get bigger
spaces as the church grows. We have live music, and a lot of what
we do isn't overtly religious. Outside we have a neon sign that says
JESUS LOVES."

Solitude has always been part of Jimmy's identity. "Practices of
solitude are in my blood. When I was eleven years old, I had a
paper route. I'd be up early each morning, on my bike, throwing
papers. I began a solitude practice then. Today, I still wake up at
five thirty each morning, while the rest of the house is asleep.
Fridays are my day off. I spend the whole day by myself until the
kids come home from school."

Jimmy grew up in Texas, where he showed a nonconformist streak early. "Everyone in my family went to SMU," he says. "It's a family tradition. But I went to UT [the University of Texas]. I got some pushback about it." After graduating from UT, Jimmy headed east, to seminary at the University of Virginia. After graduation most of his classmates went to "big churches," Jimmy says, but he went back to Austin to work for a year as a campus minister at UT. "The Episcopal priest in charge of the program said, 'You'll either be a good campus minister or our last. The program is costing us eighty thousand dollars per year, and we've only got five students involved.'" The priest asked Jimmy to think of ways to expand the program's reach. "I had gotten an intentional question from a leader I admired, about a problem I cared about," Jimmy says. "And he gave me time to think about it. I thought and prayed at my desk in the corner of the student center about my idea of a new kind of church. Eventually I had a vision in a very solitary moment—but the vision was full of people. The vision was a 'warehouse church.' That was the basic idea for Thad's."

Yet Jimmy began to follow a more traditional path after his stint as a campus minister. "To progress in my career, I needed big-church experience on my résumé. I accepted a position with a large Episcopal Church in Beverly Hills." By then Jimmy was married with one child, his son, Jass. "My son was three months old then. The opportunity felt right. L.A. matched my family's personality. We were living in a big church-owned house in Beverly Hills."

The fit turned out not to be as good as Jimmy hoped. "I wasn't comfortable there," he says. "The church has a reputation as one of the best in the Episcopal Church. But I kept asking, 'What are our metrics?' The usual ones were weekly attendance, confirmed members, contributing members." Jimmy thought those metrics were missing the point. "After a year in this system, I realized: you can do everything the church asks—attend services each week, take a leadership position, join a small group, make financial contributions—and still be a total asshole." The problem, Jimmy says, was "that we weren't getting through to these people, to call them into a deeper service in the community, our brothers and sisters outside the church."

During this time, Jimmy was part of a weekly discussion group. "It was a group of guys I met out here, all of them a little older than me. We began a conversation about entrepreneurship for the Kingdom of Heaven—what would that look like?" Jimmy missed a few meetings. When he came back, "they said, 'We've come up with our Kingdom of Heaven idea. We think we should start a church—and you should lead it.' I hadn't even told them about my warehouse church idea."

Jimmy began thinking seriously about leaving his position at the Beverly Hills church, which would mean leaving the big house that came with it. "It's important to know that Jass has very significant special needs," Jimmy says. "He's nonverbal. So during this time of formation as a priest, as a new leader, as a parent, I had a child with substantial medical and developmental issues. His father is a preacher, and he's nonverbal.

"I learned so much about communication by just living in my house," Jimmy says. "About how people communicate. People would ask me, "Does he speak?' I'd answer, 'Not English. But if you're fluent in the way he communicates, he communicates very clearly.'"

Jass's condition was at the center of Jimmy's thinking about whether to start a warehouse church. But not in the way people expected. "I'm the major breadwinner in my family," he says. "When I began stepping outside the traditional path to start Thad's, a lot of people said to me, 'This is irresponsible. You have this added responsibility to care for Jass.'" But Jimmy's reflection on his experiences as a parent made him see the situation a different way. "They were just projecting their fears onto me. Jass made my entrepreneurial side *bolder*. Having a special-needs kid blows your world away. Then you recraft it with what's left. I never would've thought I could handle this, but I'm parenting him well, I'm loving him well. What's next? I learned that you can do more than you ever thought you could, and I took that lesson to my career."

Jimmy moved forward and founded Thad's. "There aren't a lot of people in the denomination who've done what I've done," he says. Today Thad's is thriving, with a growing congregation that brings leadership challenges of its own. "As my responsibilities as a leader grow, I need more solitude," he says. "Solitude among others is my daily bread. In the park, in the house when everyone is asleep. True physical solitude is harder to accomplish in a place like L.A. I go to Wyoming three times a year, fly-fishing, climbing, hiking alone. Maybe not crossing paths with another person for two or three days. It's a feast for the soul."

Aristotle wrote, "It is by habituating ourselves to make light of alarming situations and to face them that we become brave, and it is when we have become brave that we shall most be able to face an alarming situation." Jimmy engages in that kind of habituation while facing challenges in the outdoors alone. "Adventure in the wilderness pays a positive dividend for the rest of my year," Jimmy says. "When I'm able to do things on my own in the wilderness, it translates to my work. I'm able to act in the face of fear. 'Will this program succeed or fail?' Or 'I'm afraid to disappoint this person.' But I'll move forward anyway because of the momentum I've created in solitude."

Yet Jimmy's biggest source of courage is Jass. "The deepest wound in my life," Jimmy says, "is the greatest gift."

CHAPTER 11

"A Sublime Power to Rise Above"
Winston Churchill, 1938

"I will begin, therefore, by saying the most unpopular and most
unwelcome thing."

—WINSTON CHURCHILL, OCTOBER 5, 1938

To have moral courage, a leader must be willing to sacrifice.
Sometimes the sacrifices are modest: a diminished reputation in some
quarters, questions about one's priorities in others, awkwardness in
relations that before were agreeable. Other times the sacrifices are
more serious: ostracism where once there was popularity, widespread
anger among certain groups, criticism of not only one's judgment but
one's character. Still other times the sacrifices are severe: the loss of a
job, severance of important relationships, threats of physical harm.

Consequences like these—even the modest ones—will turn
many people away from doing what they know is right. Yet there
are times when such consequences are worth bearing, because the
alternatives—misplaced priorities, harm to the organization,
compromised integrity—are worse. A leader connected with her
first principles can recognize those times and thus see that the
stakes are larger than popularity or relationships or career success.

A reflective leader will also realize she is not alone in her struggles. The leader might compare her situation to that of a past leader who faced equal or more difficult challenges, and then seek to emulate that leader. Or she might recall the example of an admired relative or friend, or of a person who suffers from disability or hardship the likes of which the leader herself has never had to face. These sources can fuse mind and soul together into a determination that transcends whatever the critics might say.

APPEASEMENT WAS NOT always a dirty word. On September 30, 1938, when Prime Minister Neville Chamberlain returned from Munich after capitulating there to all of Adolf Hitler's demands regarding Czechoslovakia, Chamberlain's countrymen greeted him as a hero. For weeks before, Europe had teetered on the brink of another Great War. But Chamberlain's Munich Agreement spared his country all that—or so he and most Britons thought. When, at the conclusion of the crisis, Chamberlain's plane landed at Heston airport outside London on the morning of September 29, Chamberlain was astounded at the size and enthusiasm of the crowd that awaited him there. Chamberlain waved his piece of paper with Hitler's signature, to the cheers of the crowd and cries of "Good old Neville!" A royal courier arrived with a message from the king, asking Chamberlain to come to Buckingham Palace and expressing "the warmest of welcomes to one who, by his patience and determination, has earned the lasting gratitude of his fellow-countrymen throughout the Empire." Chamberlain wrote afterward that "even the descriptions of the papers gives [sic] no idea of the scenes in the streets as I drove from Heston to the Palace. They were lined from one end to the other with people of every class, shouting themselves hoarse, leaping on the running board, banging on the windows and thrusting their hands into the car to be shaken." Chamberlain wrote that "the scenes culminated in Downing Street," where he opened an upstairs window at No. 10 and declared to the crowd below: "My good friends, this is the second time in our history that there has come back from Germany to Downing Street peace with honour. I believe it is peace for our time." Leo Amery, another diarist and respected House member, summarized: "For the moment the sense of escape will overshadow everything and Neville is by way of becoming not only a national but a world hero."

Yet only six days later, on October 5, 1938, Winston Churchill rose in the House of Commons and said: "I will begin, therefore, by saying the most unpopular and most unwelcome thing. I will begin by saying what everybody would like to ignore but which must nevertheless be stated, namely that we have sustained a total and unmitigated defeat." He added, "We are in the presence of a disaster of the first magnitude which has befallen Great Britain and France. Do not let us blind ourselves to that."

Churchill's speech was a supreme act of moral courage, for he was vilified—as he knew he would be—for making it. Indeed, he was taunted with cries of "Rude" and "Nonsense!" while he made it. Even members who shared Churchill's views took care after his speech not to be associated with him. And some of Churchill's own constituents from his district in Epping—loyal supporters before the speech—commenced a strong campaign to oust him from his seat. In sum, by all appearances the speech was an act of political suicide.

To UNDERSTAND WHY Churchill gave his Munich speech, one must first recall the events that led up to it. In March of 1938, Britain and France stood aside as Hitler executed his *Anschluss*— the absorption of the sovereign state of Austria—over the objections of its courageous chancellor, Kurt von Schuschnigg, and the clear majority of Austria's citizens. Then Hitler turned to Czechoslovakia. That nation was an exemplar of democracy and tolerance in central Europe, comprising ethnic Hungarians, Romanians, Slovaks, and Czechs and led by an intellectual, President Eduard Benes. For Hitler these things were bad enough. But even worse was that Czechoslovakia comprised ethnic Germans too, most of whom lived in the Sudetenland, a mountainous and heavily fortified region along Czechoslovakia's northwest border with Germany. That region, along with the formidable Czech Army, was a serious obstacle for *Fall Grun* (Case Green), which was Hitler's plan for a surprise invasion of Czechoslovakia. So Hitler and his Nazi minions fomented agitation there, manufacturing incidents of supposed Czech mistreatment of ethnic Germans. The agitation steadily escalated during the spring and summer of 1938. By September the pot had reached full boil, with brownshirt riots in the Sudetenland and screaming headlines back in Berlin, all per the Austrian model of six months before—as Churchill plainly recognized. Meanwhile, hundreds of thousands of German troops deployed along the Czech border.

The time had come, then, for what Neville Chamberlain called "Plan Z." In Chamberlain's view, the missing ingredient for stability in Europe was not greater armaments for the Western democracies, or a firmer and clearer resolve on their part to resist Nazi aggression. What was missing, rather, was what Chamberlain himself called the "Chamberlain touch." On September 13—the day after Hitler took the stage at the Nazis' annual rally at Nuremberg, to deliver a sweat-soaked tirade about "Jew plotters" and the "monstrous" Czech nation—Chamberlain decided that the time for personal diplomacy had come. That day he cabled Hitler, proposing a meeting and offering to fly to Germany as early as the next morning. Though somewhat nonplussed, Hitler accepted. Chamberlain flew to Germany on September 15, unwittingly reviewed a Death's Head SS guard upon deplaning, and then took a train to meet Hitler at Berchtesgaden. There, after minimal pleasantries, Hitler insisted at length that the *Sudetendeutsche* "return" to the Reich, stating that he was "prepared to risk a world war rather than allow this to drag on." Chamberlain could hardly get a word in edgewise. Then Hitler changed gears, venturing that a peaceful settlement was still possible if Britain agreed to a "liberation" of the Sudetenland based upon the principle of "self-determination." That was good enough for Chamberlain, who expressed his indifference as to "whether the Sudetens were in the Reich or out of it." Chamberlain asked for leave to report back to his cabinet and "secure their approval of his personal attitude." Hitler consented, and they agreed to meet the following week.

Chamberlain then reported back to his cabinet, which after some resistance agreed to his proposal to cede the Sudetenland to Germany. On September 22 Chamberlain flew to Germany to deliver this news, meeting Hitler in Godesburg. To Chamberlain's surprise, however, Hitler announced that a resolution along the lines discussed at Berchtesgaden was "no longer possible." For Hitler had decided to increase his demands: now he said that there would be no time for any process of self-determination prior to Germany's seizure of the Sudetenland. The following day, Hitler presented Chamberlain with a "memorandum" that demanded that the Czechs evacuate the Sudetenland no later than September 28—five days hence—and that the German army occupy the area beginning on September 26. Chamberlain got up to leave. Then Hitler quickly offered a "concession," which Hitler said no other man had obtained from him before. The Czechs would have an additional three days, until October 1, to clear out of the Sudetenland. That made Chamberlain comfortable again, and he bade the Führer a warm farewell.

Meanwhile the Czechs mobilized, manning their fortifications on the Sudeten frontier. On September 24 they rejected Hitler's terms. Two days later, Hitler issued an ultimatum that the Czechs accept his terms by two P.M. on September 28. By that morning the Czechs had not done so. But that same morning, through the Italians, Chamberlain proposed yet another meeting with Hitler, who promptly accepted. Chamberlain's French counterpart would also attend the meeting—in Munich.

The meeting itself was something of an anticlimax: the British and French once again agreed to Hitler's terms, but now agreed also to strong-arm the Czechs to accept them. The Czechs finally capitulated on September 30. Within days the Gestapo and SS moved in for an orgy of violence.

CHURCHILL SAW CLEARLY the demerits of Munich, even if most of his countrymen chose not to. But the clarity of Churchill's understanding was only a precondition for the speech he gave on October 5. What made the speech possible, and what gave the speech its timeless rhetorical force, was the moral power that lay behind it. And that power grew strong through Churchill's use of productive solitude.

The process was one in which Churchill engaged intensively throughout the 1930s—namely, his writing. It was a process borne of practical necessity. During the 1930s, Churchill's expenses for his residence, Chartwell Manor, and the lifestyle that came with it, were typically near $1 million annually in today's dollars. Churchill's parliamentary salary supplied less than 5 percent of that amount; most of the remainder came from Churchill's literary earnings. Thus, so far as his income was concerned, Churchill's profession was that of an author.

His output during the 1930s was prodigious. During 1930–38, he wrote a massive and critically acclaimed four-volume biography of his seventeenth-century ancestor the 1st Duke of Marlborough. From August 1938 through December 1939, Churchill dictated drafts of the first two volumes of his *History of the English-Speaking Peoples*, a total of nearly 500,000 words, including an average of 1,100 words a day during August and September 1938—the height of the Czech crisis. During this decade he also wrote a fortnightly newspaper column, hundreds of magazine articles, hundreds more speeches, and several other books.

Most of this writing occurred in Churchill's study at Chartwell, on the top floor. The room itself dates back to 1086. (Today it is preserved as it was in Churchill's time.) The doorway is Tudor. The oaken rafters and beams reach up more than twenty feet, the walls are lined with bookshelves, a fireplace lies just out of reach from Churchill's stand-up desk, and the windows provide an elevated vista of the Weald of Kent. In this room, Churchill's literary workday typically began at eleven o'clock each night. A secretary was always present to take dictation, sometimes joined by one of the young Oxford graduates who did historical research for him. But no one's presence in this room detracted from Churchill's solitude as he worked. For Churchill's concentration was total. William Manchester describes it best: "The quintessential Churchill, the Winston the public never saw, prowled his study night after night, an inner shutter drawn in a private black-out of the mind, excluding everything but the topic before him."

The effect of this solitude upon Churchill is hard to overstate. Churchill was a romantic who believed his nation was centered upon principles that—as Churchill himself might put it—were at first a distant glimmer through the primeval mists, but that, as the centuries marched forward, emerged as gleaming ideals, whose light then shone across the centuries that followed. (For Churchill, gleams and glimmers were "characteristic, elevating metaphors.") Churchill believed further that great men, possessed of the great emotion that these ideals inspire, could change the course of history—and that he was such a man. And thus, night after night, as Churchill paced back and forth across his study, he delivered not only to his readers, but to himself, a verbal history that inspired unshakable convictions within his soul.

Churchill's study of history gave him perspective as well. Churchill saw his time and his own actions in the sweep of history, whose protagonists—kings Arthur and Alfred, among others—struggled against evil and adversity in their time just as he struggled against those things in his. Their example reassured him in times of deep adversity; and the vibrancy of their legend, centuries later, revealed to him that in great adversity, there is opportunity for lasting honor and glory—that, even "if the British Empire and its Commonwealth last for a thousand years," as he put it in June 1940, his own deeds might yet be remembered.

One sees fragments of these themes roiling to the surface in 1938–39, during the months in which he was working intensively on *English-Speaking Peoples.* In a letter to the British foreign secretary, Lord Halifax, dated August 20, 1938, Churchill reported that he was "at the moment horribly entangled with the ancient Britons, the Romans, the Angles, Saxons and Jutes." In a letter to an archaeologist, dated September 19, 1938—four days after Chamberlain's first flight to meet Hitler—Churchill enclosed a draft of the section of *English-Speaking Peoples* covering the millennium before the Norman Conquest, and closed with the observation: "It has been a comfort to me in these anxious days to put a thousand years between my thoughts and the twentieth century." Reaching back yet another six hundred years, Churchill found inspiration in the example of King Arthur. After skirmishing with his research assistants as to whether the man actually existed (the assistants said not, but Churchill was indifferent, insisting that the existence of Arthur's legend alone was enough to treat him as if he did)—Churchill wrote this call to courage: "And wherever men are fighting against barbarism, tyranny, and massacre, for freedom, law, and honour, let them remember that the fame of their deeds, even though they themselves may be exterminated, may perhaps be celebrated as long as the world rolls round." Churchill himself remembered those things, because he was immersed in them almost every night in the solitude of his study at Chartwell.

Across the Channel, Churchill found a kindred spirit in the indomitable Joan of Arc. In December 1938, he wrote to his wife, Clementine: "I have just finished writing about Joan of Arc. I think she is the winner in the whole of French history." What Churchill wrote about her, just weeks after Munich, included the following: "There welled in the heart of the Maid a pity for the realm of France, sublime, perhaps miraculous, certainly invincible." In those days Churchill felt the same for England, and France too.

In Churchill's speeches shortly before Munich, one again hears echoes of his solitude. In a speech delivered May 9, 1938, he asserted: "Have we not an ideology—if we must use this ugly word—of our own in freedom, in a liberal constitution, in democratic and Parliamentary government, in Magna Charta and the Petition of Right?" And in a speech delivered August 27, 1938—"in this ancient Forest at Theydon Bois, the very name of which carries us back to Norman days"—Churchill concluded with a warning to the Germans: "Whatever may happen . . . Great Britain and the British Empire must not be deemed incapable of playing their part and doing their duty as they have done on other great occasions which have not yet been forgotten by history."

That admonition, redirected toward his own countrymen, would soon be reprised in the peroration of another speech—delivered on October 5.

CHURCHILL'S SOLITUDE WAS central to the Munich speech itself. The process of writing a complex document—for most writers, the most solitary of tasks—forces one to think much harder about its subject than does editing a document written by someone else. Churchill's Munich speech reflects this kind of clarity throughout, describing in crisp, lucid detail the calamity visited upon the Western democracies as a result of the agreement, the straightforward manner in which the calamity could have been avoided, and the consequences likely to follow. Regarding those consequences, Churchill predicted: "I venture to think that in the future the Czechoslovak state cannot be maintained as an independent entity. I think you will find that in a period of time which may be measured by years, but may be measured only by months, Czechoslovakia will be engulfed in the Nazi regime." His prediction was prophecy: Hitler's panzers rolled into Prague less than six months later, on March 15, 1939. That night Hitler declared: "Czechoslovakia has ceased to exist."

Just as the process of writing makes one think more deeply, so too can it make the writer feel more deeply. That was certainly true for Churchill. Again Manchester describes it best: "Frequently, as he dictates passages which will stir his listeners, he weeps; his voice becomes thick with emotion, tears run down his cheeks (and his secretary's)."

Churchill's Munich speech was surely one of those speeches. The papers Churchill used in preparation of his speech include a memorandum dated October 1, in which he underscored the following passage: ". . . nothing can detract from the courage and dignity [the Czechs] have displayed during the past three months." This sentiment found timeless expression in the speech itself: "All is over. Silent, mournful, abandoned, broken, Czechoslovakia recedes into the darkness." And Churchill expressed the injustice in human terms: "This particular block of land, this mass of human beings to be handed over, has never expressed the desire to go into Nazi rule."

In this speech too, one hears echoes from his Chartwell study. Churchill described Britain's fall from absolute victor in 1918 to near-vanquished twenty years later, only five years after Hitler assumed power: "We have been reduced from a position of safety and power—power to do good, power to be generous to a beaten foe, power to make terms with Germany, power to give her proper redress for her grievances, power to stop her arming if we chose, power to take any step in strength or mercy or justice which we thought right—reduced in five years from a position safe and unchallenged to where we stand now." Here Churchill found a parallel from nearly a millennium before:

> I must say that the rugged words of the *Anglo-Saxon Chronicle*, written a thousand years ago . . . apply very much to our treatment of Germany and our relations with her. "All these calamities fell upon us because of evil counsel, because tribute was not offered to them at the right time nor yet were they resisted; but when they had done the most evil, then peace was made with them." That is the wisdom of the past, for all wisdom is not new wisdom.

Churchill made his Munich speech because he was a man of principle, and because he saw so clearly the moral injustice and strategic disaster that resulted from the agreement with Hitler. But in significant part Churchill was able to make it because of the moral courage he generated in solitude. His study of history, of England's ancient ideals and all they represented, allowed him to transcend the taunts and jibes of his own age. What Churchill wrote of King Alfred, he might also have written of himself: he possessed "a sublime power to rise above the whole force of circumstances," to reach a "pinnacle of deathless glory."

Churchill closed his Munich speech with one of his most powerful perorations, and one that by no coincidence invoked the "olden time" in which he had immersed himself, night by night, for years on end.

> I do not grudge our loyal, brave people, who were ready to do their duty no matter what the cost, who never flinched under the strain of last week—I do not grudge them the natural, spontaneous outburst of joy and relief when they learned that the hard

ordeal would no longer be required of them at the moment; but they should know the truth. They should know that there has been gross neglect and deficiency in our defences; they should know that we have sustained a defeat without a war, the consequences of which will travel far with us along our road; they should know that we have passed an awful milestone in our history, when the whole equilibrium of Europe has been deranged, and that the terrible words have for the time being been pronounced against the Western democracies: "Thou art weighed in the balance and found wanting." And do not suppose that this is the end. This is only the beginning of the reckoning. This is only the first sip, the first foretaste of a bitter cup which will be proffered to us year by year unless, by a supreme recovery of moral health and martial vigour, we arise again and take our stand for freedom as in the olden time.

CHAPTER 12

"No Never Alone"
Martin Luther King Jr., 1956

"And he said, Certainly I will be with thee."
—EXODUS 3:12

There are sources of moral courage that lie latent within us. The source might be one's bond with a friend or mentor to whom one has not spoken in years—but still could call upon now. It might be an important life event whose implications one has not fully explored. It might be a relationship with a respected colleague, which, if one merely asked, could be a source of strength. When clarity about the reasons for his actions is no longer enough to sustain a leader, he can seek out these sources. What he seeks, usually, is not still more clarity about the reasons for his actions, but simply reassurance—reassurance that what he is doing is right, that he is doing his best, that he is a good person notwithstanding what the moral critics say. To sustain moral courage, a leader must tend to the soul as well as the mind. He can seek sources of reassurance by quiet reflection upon his life as a whole—the relationships that have been important to him, the things he would have done differently, the experiences that affected him most. (The second movement of Beethoven's *Emperor* concerto captures the mood of this kind of reflection.) In that quietude, and with that broader perspective, an intuition will often surface about where he can find reassurance.

Martin Luther King Jr. had the utmost clarity about the reasons for his actions as leader of the Montgomery bus boycott of 1955–56, though that role came to him unsought. And yet after two months, worn down by moral criticism and an increasing flow of hostile phone calls and death threats, King contemplated abandoning his leadership role altogether. But late one night in January 1956, when he was ready to give up, King sat down at his kitchen table and reflected on his life. Then he realized there was one relationship he could draw upon more deeply—his relationship with God, which even as a pastor he had not yet fully developed. After King stood up from that table, his courage would never leave him again.

THE GREATEST AMERICAN civil rights leader was at first a reluctant one. When Marin Luther King Jr. moved to Montgomery, Alabama, with his wife, Coretta, in September 1954, he did so to realize his career goal of becoming a pastor—a position he had accepted at the Dexter Avenue Baptist Church. He was then only twenty-five years old and had just finished studying for his doctorate at Boston University. King threw himself into his new responsibilities at Dexter, preparing a hard-nosed statement of governing principles—"Leadership never ascends from the pew to pulpit," King advised his new congregation, "but invariably descends from pulpit to pew"—in addition to spending hours each week writing and then memorizing his sermons.

Meanwhile, the Kings settled into the church's parsonage, the home provided for King as pastor. On November 17, 1955, their first child, Yolanda, was born. Around the same time, the Montgomery chapter of the NAACP—of which Rosa Parks was the secretary—offered King the chapter's presidency, having heard him deliver an impressive speech to the chapter's members a few months before. King declined, citing his responsibilities as a new pastor and father.

Only weeks later, however, leadership for King would no longer be a matter of choice. On Thursday, December 1, 1955, Rosa Parks was arrested after she refused to give up her seat to a white passenger on a bus in Montgomery. Almost immediately, the city's black leadership organized a boycott of the city's buses for the following Monday. In the meantime, two of the city's leading black activists, E. D. Nixon, an older man and a porter for a railroad company, and Ralph Abernathy, a young pastor and already a close friend of King, organized a meeting of the city's black leadership for that Friday night. Nixon called King Friday morning to ask if the meeting could be held at Dexter and to solicit King's support for the boycott. At first King hesitated: "Brother Nixon, let me think about it awhile, and call me back." Then Abernathy called King, who agreed to host the meeting and support the boycott effort so long as he "did not have to do the organizational work." At the meeting that night, the group agreed to proceed with the boycott on Monday and to distribute leaflets about the boycott over the weekend.

On Monday morning, only a handful of black passengers rode on Montgomery's buses. Meanwhile, hundreds of blacks walked to work or gathered for rides in cars driven by friends and acquaintances. The leadership group met again that afternoon. By then they had decided to create a new organization dedicated to the boycott, which at Abernathy's suggestion they named the Montgomery Improvement Association (MIA). King thought that a prominent member of his church, Rufus Lewis, should be president of the new organization. But Lewis had other ideas: at the Monday meeting, Lewis promptly nominated King for the role. As a Baptist minister who was both articulate and extremely well educated, King could appeal to all segments of the city's black community, working-class and professional alike. No other nominations were made, and King was asked if he would accept the role. After a pause, King said, "Well, if you think I can render some service, I will."

Soon thereafter, the meeting's attendees left to join a mass meeting scheduled for that evening at the Holt Street Baptist Church. As president of the MIA, King would now be the featured speaker. He stopped briefly at home, telling Coretta that he had been chosen to lead the new group. Then an old friend, Elliot Finley, picked up King to drive him to Holt Street. They ran into traffic blocks away from the church and eventually came to a halt, with people streaming past all around them. Finley parked the car. As they got out and began to walk, King paused. "You know something, Finley," King said. "This could turn into something big."

It took King fifteen minutes to push his way through the crowd to the church. One thousand people were inside, with another four thousand outside, listening to the proceedings on loudspeaker. Soon after arriving, King was called to the pulpit. For a moment he stood silently in front of the crowd, which was packed into the pews and aisles and balconies. "We are here this evening for serious business," King said. "We are here in a general sense because first and foremost we are American citizens . . . But we are here in a more specific sense because of the bus situation in Montgomery. We are here because we are determined to get the situation corrected." King described Parks's arrest and her character, saying, "Mrs. Parks is a fine Christian person, unassuming, and yet there is integrity and character there. And just because she refused to get up, she was arrested."

"And you know, my friends," King continued, "there comes a time when people get tired of being trampled over by the iron feet of oppression." At that, a rising cheer suddenly exploded into deafening applause, rolling on and on, "like a wave that refused to break, and just when it seemed that the roar must finally weaken, a wall of sound came in from the enormous crowd outdoors to push the volume still higher"—all the while with the thunder of feet stomping on the wooden floor. Finally, King said, "We are here, we are here this evening because we're tired now."

The church was humming now. "And we are not wrong, we are not wrong in what we are doing." King began to belt out the words. "If we are wrong, the Supreme Court of this nation is wrong. If we are wrong, the Constitution of the United States is wrong. If we are wrong, God Almighty is wrong!" Again the crowd exploded. "If we are wrong, Jesus of Nazareth was merely a utopian dreamer and never came down to earth! If we are wrong, justice is a lie." For a while he could not speak because of the thunderous applause. Then, quoting from the book of Amos, he said, "And we are determined here in Montgomery to work and fight 'until justice runs down like water, and righteousness like a mighty stream!'" He began to conclude. "Love is one of the pinnacle parts of the Christian faith. There is another side called justice. And justice is really just love in calculation. Justice is love correcting that which would work against love." He called the crowd to action. "Right here in Montgomery, when the history books are written in the future," he said, they will say that here was "a people who had the moral courage to stand up for their rights." Then he abruptly closed, saying, "Let us think on these things."

When King was done, Ralph Abernathy rose to read a resolution calling for everyone to continue the boycott until a satisfactory arrangement was reached with the city's white leadership. The crowd roared its approval. As King walked out of the church, with the applause continuing all around, people reached out to touch him. In the course of a single afternoon and evening, King had gone from a hesitant participant in the boycott to its indisputable leader.

THE MIA'S LEADERSHIP thought the city would give in after a week or so at most. Part of the reason for their optimism was the modesty of their demands: the black leadership was not, to the disappointment of the national NAACP, seeking full integration of the city's buses. The current seating system had a whites-only section toward the front of the buses, a blacks-only section toward the back, and sixteen seats in the middle, where the bus driver would shift the line between the races depending on how the racial composition of the riders might shift. In practice, however, the line shifted only backward, with the bus driver ordering black passengers to move to the rear as additional seats were needed for whites. Moreover, seated whites were never directed to stand to make room for new black passengers, whereas blacks were often ordered to stand to make room for boarding whites. (Hence the driver's directive to Rosa Parks and a handful of other black passengers on

December 1: "I want those two seats.") What the MIA demanded was simply the same seating plan that the same bus company, National City Lines, used on its buses in Mobile, Alabama: neither race would have a reserved section, whites would seat themselves from the front, blacks from the back, and the dividing line between the races would be wherever they happened to meet.

Yet the MIA's optimism soon began to fade. On December 8— one week after Parks's arrest—King led a delegation of black leaders in a meeting with the city's three commissioners and the bus company's lawyer, Jack Crenshaw. When King proposed that the company adopt the Mobile plan in Montgomery, Crenshaw responded, implausibly, that the state's segregation law prohibited that approach. Perhaps more to the point, Crenshaw also objected that, under the MIA's plan, a black male passenger could be "practically rubbing knees" with a white woman. The meeting went nowhere. The two groups met again on December 17, this time joined by three white ministers, who lectured King about the impropriety of "ministers of the gospel leading a political campaign." That meeting too went nowhere.

Meanwhile, the MIA's leadership began the formidable task of creating a private carpool system for the thousands of black residents who had used the city's buses. Eventually almost every black-owned car in the city was volunteered for the effort. Even discounting for the black residents who now walked instead of rode to their destinations, however, each car in the effort would need to provide around a hundred rides per day. A similar system had broken down in Baton Rouge after only two weeks. For the time being though, Montgomery's black residents each found ways to get back and forth to work, and to the grocery store, and to the MIA's now-frequent mass meetings, while also keeping up with all the other obligations of daily life.

At this point the pressure on King began to grow more acute. With the prospects of a quick settlement now dim and logistical difficulties increasing for the MIA, the black and white delegations met for a third time on December 19. Joining them this time, to the blacks' dismay, was Luther Ingalls, secretary of the

Montgomery chapter of the White Citizens Council, a pro-segregation group. When Ingalls began to speak a few minutes into the meeting, King objected, looking directly at Ingalls and saying that some of the whites present had "preconceived ideas" and their "minds already made up." That in turn angered some of the more open-minded whites. Trembling with indignation, Mrs. Logan Hipp told King, "I resent very deeply the statement that we have come here with preconceived ideas. I most certainly did not." A white businessman added that he had come "prepared to vote for liberalization of interpretation of the city's laws with certain conditions. We have some whose minds are made up and I think Reverend King is one of them." Taken aback, King explained that he thought only some of the whites were biased. The chairman of the white delegation, the Reverend Henry Parker, retorted that, "if that's true, then *you* should not be here. Your stand has been made clear." King was speechless, and no one else spoke. "For a moment," King recalled later, "it appeared that I was alone. Nobody came to my rescue." Then Ralph Abernathy stood up and said that King spoke for all the members of the black delegation. A short while later the meeting came to a bitter end.

Afterward, King felt what he described as a "terrible sense of guilt." He feared that his outburst had ruined the negotiations, just as the boycott's burdens grew heavier for the city's black community. King was also dismayed at the perception, among the white delegation at least, that his comments had put the whites on the moral high ground. Later that day he called Reverend Parker to apologize. Parker was taken aback at the gesture, which suggested equality, and nervously repeated the points he had made in the meeting that day.

In the days that followed, the city's white leadership described King as the primary obstacle to a settlement, and wondered aloud "why the older, long-established leaders of black Montgomery had ceded authority to this young newcomer." Whites also began a whispering campaign that King was skimming from donations made to the MIA. King "almost broke down from the continual battering," he said later. At an emotional meeting of the MIA's

160 LEAD YOURSELF FIRST

board, King offered to resign. The board rejected the offer and instead rallied around him.

Meanwhile the whites' position hardened. On January 6, Police Commissioner Clyde Sellers—an ardent segregationist—strode down the aisle of a 1,200-person meeting of the Montgomery White Citizens Council and announced that he was joining the organization. He received a standing ovation. Afterward the city's leading newspaper, the *Montgomery Advertiser*, reported that, "in effect, the Montgomery police force is now an arm of the White Citizens Council." Also on January 6, the Montgomery city attorney wrote to a state solicitor, arguing that the MIA's actions violated a state anti-boycott law. And membership in the Montgomery White Citizens Council was surging, from three hundred the previous October to six thousand by the end of January. At the same time, the MIA's carpool system was strained to the limit, and the MIA itself was nearly out of funds.

The MIA began looking for a way out. King requested a meeting with Sellers and the city's three commissioners, which took place on January 9. This time the MIA's attorney, Fred Gray—rather than King—spoke for the black delegation. Gray offered the whites a major concession, namely that black passengers would voluntarily reseat themselves to the rear of buses as necessary to make room for boarding white passengers. (Theoretically whites would do the same for black passengers, though no one expected that to happen in practice.) Sensing weakness, the white delegation rejected the proposal out of hand.

Three days later, at an MIA board meeting, the mood was gloomy. The group concluded, "It seems that it is now a test as to which side can hold out the longer time, or wear the other down." The group also noted that the national NAACP would not support their efforts unless the MIA abandoned its seating plan and instead sought full integration of the buses through litigation. The board began discussions about whether to file suit in federal court.

For King, the pressures at this point became even more intensely personal. Day and night his home phone rang with calls, sometimes from blacks complaining about some aspect of the carpool, but more often from hostile whites, some making death threats. On January 19, the *Advertiser* ran a front-page article with the headline THE REV. KING IS BOYCOTT BOSS. A citywide rumor campaign followed, with whites saying to black acquaintances that King was an ambitious, "highfalutin preacher" who had never ridden a bus himself.

Soon King also found himself caught up in a campaign of police harassment. On January 22, presumably at Sellers's direction, Montgomery police began pulling over carpool drivers wherever they saw them, issuing tickets for equipment violations and bogus charges of speeding or failure to signal. On January 26, King was driving home from work along with several passengers. A pair of police motorcycles began to tail behind. King slowed to a crawl, but the motorcycles continued to follow. When King stopped to let out some passengers, one of the officers pulled up next to the driver's window. "Get out, King," the officer said. "You're under arrest for speeding 30 miles an hour in a 25-mile zone." Stunned, King told a remaining passenger to notify Coretta. Then he stepped out of the car. The officers called for a cruiser and put King in the backseat. The officers said nothing as they drove through unfamiliar, desolate parts of town. King silently began to panic, literally trembling in the backseat, seized with fear that he was about to be lynched. But eventually they approached a building with a neon sign outside: MONTGOMERY CITY JAIL. Inside, King was led toward a large cell filled with common criminals. "All right, get on in there with all the others," the jailer said. A while later, the jailer returned for him. King thought he was being released, but instead he was fingerprinted and returned to the cell. Ralph Abernathy came to the jail and then ran off to get money for a cash bond. As a crowd of black supporters began to gather outside the jail, however, the jailers released King upon his own signature. That night no fewer than seven mass meetings were held at different black churches.

The following night—January 27, 1956—King came home very late from work. "It was the most important night of his life," says King's Pulitzer-winning biographer, David Garrow, "the one he would always think back to in future years when the pressures again seemed too great."

The house was quiet, and Coretta and Yolanda were already asleep. By then King was reaching his emotional limits. "I felt myself faltering and growing in fear," he said later. Around midnight, he began to prepare for bed. Then the phone rang. The white on the other end of the line called King the N-word and told him, "We are tired of you and your mess now. And if you aren't out of this town in three days, we're going to blow your brains out, and blow up your house."

King had gotten death threats before, but this time something broke loose inside him. Fearful and unable to sleep, he went to the kitchen, made a cup of coffee, and sat down at the table to reflect. "I started thinking about many things," he said later. "I was ready to give up."

> I sat there and thought about a beautiful little daughter who had just been born. . . . I'd come in night after night and see that little gentle smile. And I sat at that table thinking about that little girl and thinking about the fact that she could be taken away from me any minute.
>
> And I started thinking about a dedicated, devoted, and loyal wife, who was over there asleep. And she could be taken from me, or I could be taken from her. And I got to the point that I couldn't take it any longer. I was weak. Something said to me, you can't call on Daddy now, he's up in Atlanta 175 miles away. You can't even call on Mama now. You've got to call on that something in that person that your Daddy used to tell you about, the power that can make a way out of no way.

At that point King realized that he needed to draw more deeply on his faith than ever before:

> And I discovered then that religion had become real to me, and I had to know God for myself. And I bowed down over that cup of coffee. I will never forget it . . . I prayed a prayer, and I prayed out loud that night. I said, "Lord, I'm down here trying to do what's right. I think I'm right. I think the cause that we represent

is right. But Lord, I must confess that I'm weak now. I'm faltering. I'm losing my courage. And I can't let the people see me like
this because if they see me weak and losing my courage, they will
begin to get weak."

Then King received his answer:

> And it seemed at that moment that I could hear an inner voice
> saying to me, "Martin Luther, stand up for righteousness. Stand
> up for justice. Stand up for truth. And lo I will be with you, even
> until the end of the world" . . . I heard the voice of Jesus saying
> still to fight on. He promised never to leave me, never to leave me
> alone. No never alone. No never alone. He promised never to
> leave me, never to leave me alone.

"Almost at once," King said later, "my fears began to go. My uncertainty disappeared."

Never again would he fear bombings, or any other harm his
adversaries could do to him.

THREE DAYS LATER, on the night of January 30, Coretta was
sitting with a friend in the front room of the parsonage when they
heard an object land on the porch outside. They darted toward a
guest bedroom as "an explosion rocked the house, filling the front
room with smoke and shattered glass." When King heard the
news, he rushed home to find an angry crowd of supporters outside.
Police Commissioner Sellers and the city's mayor were already
there. Sellers took King aside and told him, "I do not agree with
you in your beliefs, but I will do everything within my power to
defend you against such acts as this." Then King sought to calm
the crowd. Raising up one hand for silence, he said, "Everything is
all right . . . everything is under control." He urged the onlookers
not to retaliate. "We are not advocating violence. We want to love
our enemies. I want you to love our enemies. Be good to them.
Love them and let them know you love them." Reflecting later,
King said he had "accepted the word of the bombing calmly. My

religious experience a few nights before had given me the strength to face it."

Eventually the MIA filed its lawsuit challenging segregation on Montgomery's buses as unconstitutional. On June 5, 1956, a divided three-judge panel (with Judge Frank Johnson in the majority) held that that it was. On November 1, 1956, the Supreme Court allowed that decision to stand. The city sought rehearing, which the Court denied on December 20. The following day, segregation on the city's buses came to an end.

But King's challenges as a leader did not. Exactly one year after his experience at the kitchen table, another stack of dynamite landed on the porch of his home. The fuse was defective and the bomb did not explode. In his sermon the next morning, a Sunday, King again described his religious experience a year earlier, and said, "So I'm not afraid of anybody this morning. Tell Montgomery they can keep shooting and I'm going to stand up to them; tell Montgomery they can keep bombing and I'm going to stand up to them."

For the rest of his short life, King had a strong sense that he would one day be killed in the service of his cause. Because of his experience at the kitchen table, however, he faced that prospect without fear. And though King did not speak of it directly, he was surely aware of a scriptural parallel to his own experience. In the Book of Exodus, God speaks to Moses through the burning bush and orders him to return to Egypt and lead his people to freedom. Moses reacts with self-doubt: "Who am I, that I should go unto Pharaoh, and that I should bring forth the children of Israel out of Egypt?" God responds, "Certainly I will be with thee" (Exodus 3:11–12).

King had been told the same thing. And he knew that the parallel went a step further. Black Americans have long identified with the Israelites of the Old Testament, who were persecuted by the pharaoh. After Moses leads the Israelites out of Egypt, they wander the desert for forty years. Finally God tells Moses to "get thee up this mountain," from whose top God says he will allow Moses to see the Promised Land. And God says he will give this land "unto the children of Israel for a possession" (Deuteronomy 32:48–49). But God will not let Moses himself go there; instead, God says, Moses will die on the mountain. Moses then climbs up the mountain, sees the Promised Land, and dies.

And so, on April 3, 1968, King's audience would have understood his meaning entirely. Before a black congregation in Memphis, King ended the last speech of his life this way:

> Well, I don't know what will happen now. We've got some difficult days ahead. But it really doesn't matter with me now, because I've been to the mountaintop. And I don't mind. Like anybody, I would like to live a long life. Longevity has its place. But I'm not concerned about that now. I just want to do God's will. And He's allowed me to go up to the mountain, and I've looked over, and I've seen the Promised Land. I may not get there with you. But I want you to know tonight, that we, as a people will get to the Promised Land. And so I'm happy tonight. I'm not fearing any man. Mine eyes have seen the glory of the coming of the Lord.

King's sense from his experience at the kitchen table, that the Lord was with him each step of the way, had grown into a deeper sense that, as with Moses, the Lord himself would decide when his work was done.

And the following morning, it was.

CHAPTER 13

The Dignity Not to Conform
Pope John Paul II, 1979

"The real danger to both sides—for the Church and the other side, call it what you will—is the man who does not . . . listen to his deepest convictions, to his inner truth, but who wants only to fit, to float in conformity . . . The future of Poland will depend on how many people are mature enough to be nonconformist."

—POPE JOHN PAUL II, JUNE 1979

In times of shared sacrifice, a leader must inspire moral courage in his followers as well as in himself. In such times the leader's responsibilities are especially great, for a leader's first obligation is to take care of his people. If he cannot provide for them in material ways, he must provide for their spirit. To do so requires humility: although the leader has more power than his followers, he must recognize that as to the things that govern human worth—dignity, character, decency—his station counts for nothing. He must hold the conviction that, as to these things, he is not above his followers, but among them. For only then can he speak to these things in ways that inspire his followers.

Yet for many leaders humility is difficult to come by. Like most people, leaders are prone to self-admiration. And a leader might hear every day—sometimes directly, sometimes in ways more oblique—that his ideas are insightful, his jokes funny, even that he is virtuous. Sometimes the praise is sincere, sometimes not; but in either case the leader who takes it seriously will allow himself to be convinced, though he might not say it aloud, that his admirers indeed have a point. And then he will begin to set himself above his followers.

Honest reflection can deflate these pretensions. A leader who is connected with her first principles can reflect on the ways she has fallen short of meeting them. And she can reflect on the ways that many of the people she encounters in daily life—the people who work for her, especially in more modest positions: the waiter who does his work cheerfully, even though the people he serves are not always cheerful in return; the maid who cleaned her hotel room that morning, and who gets up early each morning to clean other rooms all day—are at least her equals as measured by those same principles. A leader who demonstrates this kind of respect for her followers can speak to them with credibility about their common values. She will also have a deeper understanding of what those common values mean. And thus she can inspire them.

Such were the practices of Pope John Paul II, as he inspired his people to resist the oppressions of communism.

IN JUNE 1979, during his first visit as pope to millions of Poles suffering under totalitarian rule, John Paul II said that "every cross placed on someone's shoulders acquires a dignity that is humanly inconceivable." That insight was borne of a lifetime of crosses. The pope was born as Karol Wojtyla (pronounced Voy-*tee*-wah) in Wadowice, Poland, in 1920. From an early age he experienced great loss. His only sister died when she was an infant; his mother died when Wojtyla was nine; and his only brother, a doctor, died of scarlet fever after treating patients with the same disease when Wojtyla was twelve. That left Wojtyla and his father alone as the surviving members of their family. Eight years later, on September 1, 1939, after attending morning Mass in Krakow, he heard the wail of German Stuka dive-bombers (the planes were equipped with sirens to make their attacks more terrifying) as they descended almost vertically to bomb the town. For the next two weeks Wojtyla and his father were refugees: first they moved east to flee the Germans, but then turned back after the Soviet Army invaded from that direction. The two Wojtylas returned to their small apartment near Krakow, where the Gestapo soon took control. During the harsh winter of 1940–41—with a food ration amounting to nine hundred calories per day, most of it from potatoes—Wojtyla shoveled broken limestone into railcars at the bottom of the Zakrzowek quarry each day, often in temperatures as low as –22 degrees Fahrenheit. Then, in 1942, his beloved father died; Wojtyla said later that "I never felt so alone." And in 1945, for Wojtyla and those around him, life under Gestapo rule transitioned almost without interruption to life under totalitarian communist rule. By the late 1940s, the communist regime had interned or murdered tens of thousands of political prisoners, suppressed freedom of expression, established a web of informants that reached every neighborhood and parish in the land, and eliminated almost every institution capable of crystallizing opposition to communist rule. The Catholic Church in Poland was an exception, but only a partial one. The Church's autonomy was restricted, and every priest and church official, Wojtyla included, had his own watcher and secret-police file. Yet from these experiences, over two decades of prayer and deep reflection, Wojtyla came to articulate a vision of human dignity that would play an essential role in bringing freedom to Poland and beyond.

From his earliest years as an adult, Wojtyla made solitude an integral part of his spiritual and intellectual life. As a young priest in his thirties, Wojtyla took students on skiing or camping trips in the Polish mountains, but just as often went alone. Of the Tatra Mountains in southern Poland, a friend said that there was not a single one "that has not been climbed or skied by Karol Wojtyla." When students did accompany him camping, Wojtyla would awaken at dawn each morning and slip away in his kayak for an hour's paddle alone. When hiking, Wojtyla would drift to the rear of the group at the end of each day for an hour or two of solitude, his face distant in contemplation and prayer. The students called him *Wujek*, or Uncle, for in those years such trips with a priest were forbidden in Communist Poland; and they would tease him about his tendency to "switch off," or suddenly draw inward, while in the midst of some activity. (One student recalled that they would not let *Wujek* lead the group while bicycling, for fear that he would ride into a tree.) And years later, as Archbishop of Krakow, Wojtyla "often took his most difficult decisions to the shrine at Kalwaria Zebrzydowska," a bucolic network of small chapels among wooded paths, where he would walk for hours alone in contemplation.

DESPITE THE ADVERSITY of his early life, as a young priest Wojtyla had some positive examples to reflect upon. One was his father, whose dignity and character were a model for Wojtyla throughout his life. The elder Karol Wojtyla had been a noncommissioned officer in the Hapsburg Army and was known to everyone in Wadowice as "the captain." A man of intelligence, piety, and "granite integrity," the elder Wojtyla bore suffering with quiet courage. He was also a notably decent man, whose goodwill extended not only to the town's Catholics but also to its Jews, who then made up one-fifth of the town's residents. That embrace of other faiths passed fully to his son: when his high-school classmates divided into Catholic and Jewish soccer teams, young Karol, as often as not, chose to play for the Jews. And many years later, on his first full day as pope, the first friend that John Paul brought in to see him was his high-school classmate Jerzy Kluger—who was Jewish. In this respect, among many others, Karol said that his father's "example was in a way my first seminary, a kind of domestic seminary."

Wojtyla was also deeply impressed by the dignity of the men with whom he labored in the Zakrzowek quarry. These men were largely uneducated and bore terrible burdens of their own, but they treated the young Wojtyla with sympathy, encouraging him where they could and allowing him to warm himself in a small hut with an iron stove. From these men Wojtyla learned that even the worst drudgery, when borne without self-pity, can be a source of dignity. Wojtyla reflected on the experience two decades later, in a poem called "The Quarry." He wrote: "The whole greatness of this work dwells inside a man."

In October 1941 Wojtyla was transferred to the Solvay chemical factory, where he hauled buckets of lime in the plant's water-purification unit. There, the other workers covered for him while he surreptitiously read forbidden religious texts during the night shift. After years of working with such men, the proletariat would never be for Wojtyla the abstraction it was for the communists. As Wojtyla later wrote of these men, he knew "their living situations, their families, their interests," and above all "their human worth."

To respect the worth of others relative to oneself is to be humble. Wojtyla's respect for the worth of the men at Zakrzowek and Solvay deepened his humility. In the late 1940s, as a pastor in rural Poland, east of Krakow, Wojtyla rode from village to village in a horse cart. When summoned while on vacation to meet the primate of Poland (the nation's highest Catholic official), Wojtyla hitched a ride in a milk truck, riding in back among the bottles. Years later, as archbishop of Krakow—a position second only to the primate's— Wojtyla opened his office at eleven A.M. each day to anyone who came to meet him, no appointment required. Typically he would invite a visitor to join him for lunch. Wojtyla's material poverty was of a piece. His clothes were usually threadbare, and for years he wore an old green coat made out of material for blankets. His only possessions were a framed photograph of his parents and a few books he used for work. In all his life, he never had a bank account; and if anyone gave him money or some other gift, Wojtyla would give it away to some needy person the same day.

To these qualities Wojtyla joined a superlative intellect; he received a doctorate in theology with nearly the highest possible marks from Jagiellonian University in 1948. He also displayed a remarkable aptitude for sustained analytical thinking—the ability not only to think deeply, but to do so for lengthy periods of time— which is itself a trait strengthened in solitude. And Wojtyla had a gift for intuition about the human condition. He was also a mystic, a man whose most powerful emotional and spiritual experiences took place in a realm beyond words. Taken together, when the Polish government began to crack down in earnest on religious freedom in the mid-1950s, Wojtyla's qualities would make him a formidable opponent.

THE VATICAN SOON appreciated Wojtyla's abilities. In 1958 Pope Pius XII named Wojtyla a bishop, making him at age thirty-eight the youngest in Poland. And only five years later, Pope Paul VI—a man who respected Wojtyla enough to view him as a potential successor—named Wojtyla the archbishop of Krakow, then a diocese of 1.5 million Catholics, including 1,500 priests. The Krakovian diocese is steeped in Polish history: since the eleventh century the archbishop has been known as the *defensor populi*, "defender of the people," and *defensor civitatis*, "defender of the city"—defending both of these things, when necessary, from the tyrannical power of the state. Two decades before, Archbishop Adam Stefan Sapieha—aristocratic, iron-willed, a man beyond intimidation—had served fearlessly in those roles during the Nazi occupation, even after his superior, the primate, had fled the country. Sapieha had ordained Wojtyla a priest in 1946; now, as archbishop himself, Wojtyla would confront a different tyranny.

By then Wojtyla had drawn intense interest from the Polish secret police, known as the SB (or Sluzba Bezpieczenstwai). For twenty years—from 1958 to the day he became pope—SB agents tailed Wojtyla's every move, twenty-four hours a day, 365 days a year. They also tapped his phone and bugged his residences with listening devices; when Wojtyla had sensitive Church business to discuss, he took a walk outside. The SB made a special effort to recruit Wojtyla's associates, and by 1967 some 270 of them were informing against him. Predictably, then, Wojtyla was routinely the subject of SB memoranda, many of which were shared with the East German Stasi and the Soviet KGB. One memo, prepared in 1960, said that Wojtyla merged an "unusual combination of intellectual qualities with those of an active, practical, and organized man"; that he was "very approachable, obliging, and responsible," "not easily influenced" but "willing to take advice"; that he was "not at all superficial," but a "devout man in a more rational and 'metaphysical' way than an emotional one"; and that—problematically for the communists—he was "a man of integrity." The SB's conclusion in a later memo was more sinister: "Wojtyla is a very dangerous ideological opponent."

What made Wojtyla so dangerous was the genuinely profound thought that he had given to the premises underlying the regime. Wojtyla made a point to set aside time for that kind of thinking in his daily routine. As archbishop, every morning after Mass and then breakfast, Wojtyla closed the door behind him in his chapel and spent two hours thinking and writing at a small desk alone. During those hours, "writing in the solitude of his chapel," Wojtyla produced "numerous philosophical essays and three books, as well as a stream of pastoral letters, sermons, poems, and a play." And from those works, and the thinking that lay behind them, Wojtyla developed a thorough critique that would ultimately break apart the foundations of the communist regime.

The communists inculcated a vision of man as spiritually empty, with the decisions of each person determined by economic forces rather than free will. The regime promised to liberate Poles from those forces, and thus posed as "the true champion of human freedom." Better than any other observer in Poland, however, Wojtyla understood that the communists' goal was to denude Poles of their individuality—by disabling or corrupting their consciences, and by, as a matter of survival, making the state their first and only allegiance. The result was what the Czech playwright Václav Havel later called the communist "culture of the lie." (A Polish joke from the era illustrated the point: "Party boss: 'How much is 2 + 2?' Polish worker: 'How much would you like it to be?'") The communists' goal was to deny Poles the ability to form moral courage—and by doing so to deprive them of the ability to resist.

Wojtyla responded with what he later called "Living in the Truth." His critique had two themes, one about the nature of man, the other about Polish cultural history. Drawing upon his writings as archbishop—notably, his ethical treatise *Person and Act*—Wojtyla argued that man is intrinsically drawn to truth, goodness, and beauty. But Wojtyla also argued that man possesses free will, and thus can choose between good and evil, noble and base. Wrong choices are therefore "an integral part of the truth about man." Man's dignity comes in the struggle to make good choices—as the men in the Zakrzowek quarry had made in the kindness they showed Wojtyla and each other. No economic determinism drove them to that. And if those men, under those conditions, could choose a path of dignity, so could Poles now. Hence the admonition Wojtyla always made after talking over a problem brought to him by a parishioner or friend: "*You* must decide." Wojtyla sought to reawaken Poles' awareness of their free will, and by doing so to restore their dignity and their ability to form moral courage.

Wojtyla's second theme was cultural. Just as Churchill saw English history as punctuated by leaders who fought against tyranny, Wojtyla saw the same pattern in Polish history, except that the leaders were clergy and the freedom for which they fought was religious. The most important in this tradition was St. Stanislaw, Wojtyla's earliest predecessor as bishop of Krakow (as Wojtyla was acutely aware), who in 1079 was slain for defending religious liberty against a tyrannical king. The line stretched all the way forward to Archbishop Sapieha and included Father Maximilian Kolbe, who while interned at Auschwitz had given his life—by volunteering to be placed in a "starvation cell," where he was left without food or water until, days later, in agony, he died—to save the life of another prisoner. This tradition of heroic resistance in turn formed the core of Polish cultural identity, which the Poles had preserved even during the many years—such as 1795 to 1919 and 1940 to 1945—when Poland had disappeared as an independent state. In those years, the Poles had a culture without a nation; now, under communist rule, they had a nation that denied its culture, that sought to erase this tradition from the pages of Polish history. Soon Wojtyla would wield that tradition of Polish heroism, and the truths about man that lay behind it, as powerful weapons of resistance against the communist regime.

* * *

WOJTYLA'S RESISTANCE TO communist rule took many forms, but its centerpiece during his years as archbishop was his fight to build a church in Nowa Huta. Located, by no coincidence, less than ten miles from Krakow, Nowa Huta was a "model city" built from the ground up as an embodiment of communist ideals. Its long, dreary blocks of apartment buildings were themselves a physical denial of individualism. They were also a denial of what, in *Person and Act*, Wojtyla called "solidarity," a community of individuals who support one another as they strive to live with dignity. In these buildings there was no access to neighboring units; "to visit the adjacent apartment, one had to go down to the ground floor, exit the building, and go in by another entrance— thus facilitating the work of secret police surveillance." But most importantly the city lacked a church, the keystone of Polish cultural identity. Wojtyla understood perfectly the statement that the country's rulers sought to make in Nowa Huta. Quite literally, the city was a concrete denial of man's nature and the Polish cultural tradition, and beginning in 1958 Wojtyla began a campaign to build a church there. Year after year, the regime rejected Wojtyla's application for a building permit. But year after year, Wojtyla brought an expression of humanity to Nowa Huta nonetheless. For almost two decades, every Christmas, Wojtyla performed Midnight Mass in an open field in Nowa Huta, in front of a thousand people standing on the sharp, uneven ground of a frozen marsh, the winter winds howling metaphorically around them, all of it a statement of their humanity and resistance to communist rule. Eventually the regime gave in and allowed the city's residents to build the Ark Church. Completed in 1977, the church is a strikingly modern structure, reaching dramatically upward, its exterior covered with two million individual stones made smooth by the rivers of Poland. Now the city had a structure that offered a competing vision of man.

Two years later, Wojtyla leveraged the effects of his solitude on the grandest scale. On October 3, 1978, as archbishop of Krakow, Wojtyla had flown from Poland to Rome to join a conclave to select a successor to John Paul I. Thirteen days later Wojtyla himself was pope, and as a result no longer at liberty to return to Poland. But the Polish communists understood (even as Soviet leader Leonid Brezhnev did not) that they had no choice but to allow John Paul II to visit Poland before long. (Brezhnev advised otherwise: "Tell the Pope—he's a wise man—he can declare publicly that he can't come due to illness.") Wojtyla was the first non-Italian elected pope in 455 years, the first Slav ever elected, and the first Pole. Few had seen his election coming, and it sent shock waves through the communist bloc—just as in every city and town in Poland it sent church bells ringing and people pouring into the streets, waving Polish flags, crying, embracing strangers, filling churches, for those hours bearing joyful witness to all that Wojtyla had said about them in the decades before.

John Paul II returned to Poland on the morning of June 2, 1979, and kissed the ground as soon as he stepped off the gangway of the plane. That afternoon, he stood before a million Poles in Victory Square in Warsaw. In front of him was the tomb of the Unknown Soldier. Behind was a thirty-foot-high wooden cross. There, Karol Wojtyla delivered what his most accomplished biographer, George Weigel, says "may have been the greatest sermon of his life." During the sermon—and the entire "Nine Days" of his visit—Wojtyla never referred directly to the Polish government, whose leaders that day watched from hotel balconies along the square. But he did speak about the truths, about man and Poland, that would in time bring down the regime. He began by emphasizing the extraordinary moment in Polish history of which they were all a part: just one month after the nine-hundredth anniversary of Stanislaw's death, a Pole stood before them as pope. Wojtyla's "own pilgrimage to the motherland," he said, was "surely a special sign of the pilgrimage that we Poles are making down through the history of the Church" and "of Europe and the world." He asked "why, precisely in 1978," after centuries of popes from another country, "a son of the Polish Nation, of the land of Poland, was called to the chair of St. Peter." Christ had demanded of Peter and the apostles that they be his witnesses "'to the end of the earth.' Have we not the right," Wojtyla said, "to think that Poland has become nowadays the land of a *particularly responsible* witness?" If so, Poland at that moment stood at a crossroads in history. "But if we accept all that I have dared to affirm in this moment, how many great duties and obligations arise? Are we capable of them?" The crowd began to chant: "We want God, we want God . . ."

Then—like Churchill in his study as he wrote his Munich speech—Wojtyla put the present crisis in the sweep of national history. In a challenge to communist orthodoxy, he said that "Christ cannot be kept out of the history of man in any part of the globe, at any longitude or latitude of geography. The exclusion of Christ from the history of man is an act against man." And about Poland, he said, "it is impossible without Christ to understand this nation with its past so full of splendor and also of terrible difficulties." Christ was the animating force of Polish history, from "Stanislaw in Skalka to Maximilian Kolbe at Auschwitz" to the Warsaw uprising in 1944. And he prayed that "Jesus Christ does not cease to be an ever open book on man, his dignity and his rights and also a book of knowl-edge on the dignity and rights of the nation."

He then spoke about sacrifice, and by implication the suffering his listeners were enduring under their government now. "We are before the tomb of the Unknown Soldier . . . On how many battle-fields has that soldier given witness to the rights of man, indelibly inscribed in the rights of the people, for our freedom and yours." Were those sacrifices—and the sacrifices of the people now before him—in vain? He made clear they were not.

> I wish to kneel beside this tomb and to venerate every seed that falls into the earth and dies and thus bears fruit. It may be the seed of the blood of a soldier shed on the battlefield, or the sacri-fice of martyrdom in concentration camps or in prisons. It may be the seed of hard daily toil, with the sweat of one's brow, in the fields, the workshop, the mine, the foundries and the factories. It may be the seed of the love of parents who do not refuse to give life to a new human being and undertake the whole task of bringing him up . . . It may be the seed of prayer, of service to the sick, the suffering—"all that of which Poland is made."

All of these things—all of the sacrifices made "by each son and daughter of the motherland, even if they are anonymous and unknown like the Soldier before whose tomb we are now"; all of "the history of the peoples that have lived with us and among us, such as those who died in their hundreds of thousands in the Warsaw ghetto"; all "that I now embrace in thought and in my heart during this Eucharist"—all of these things, he said, are joined with the "most holy Sacrifice of Christ, on Victory Square."

And having thus offered all the sacrifices the Polish nation had borne during the terrible century in which he spoke, and during the centuries before, Wojtyla closed with a prayer on behalf of all Poland.

> And I cry—I who am a Son of the land of Poland and who am
>   also Pope John Paul II—I cry from all the depths of this
>   Millennium, I cry on the vigil of Pentecost:
> Let your Spirit descend.
> Let your Spirit descend,
> and renew the face of this earth,
> the face of *this* land.
> Amen.

Wojtyla's sermon was the culmination of a lifetime of prayer and reflection about man and suffering and the particular struggle in which the Polish nation found itself then. And when he was done, he had made clear a "crucial truth" for the millions of people who heard him. As Weigel puts it: "Poland was not a communist country," Poland was a Catholic country saddled for the time being "with a communist state."

The days that followed brought an emotional outpouring un-rivaled in the nation's history. On June 7 the pope traveled to Auschwitz, where he stood silently in the doorway of Maximilian Kolbe's starvation cell, then kneeled in prayer and kissed the cement floor. Later he walked slowly along the line of twenty-one inscriptions to the victims of Auschwitz, each of the inscriptions in the victims' own language. "In particular," he said, "I pause . . .

before the inscription in Hebrew . . . The very people who received from God the commandment, 'You shall not kill,' itself experienced in a special measure what is meant by killing. It is not permissible to pass by this inscription with indifference."

The next day John Paul traveled to Skalka, the site of Stanislaw's death nine hundred years before. That night he spoke to a gathering of tens of thousands of students and youths. Until then the audiences to which he spoke had been notable above all for their dignity. But emotions had been building throughout the week, and now the youths before him reached a "fever pitch" of enthusiasm. Setting aside his prepared remarks, for a while the pope was unable to speak above the singing and commotion. When things calmed down somewhat, he simply said, "I love you all." For a while he bantered back and forth with the crowd, until a stillness came over them. Then, in the darkness, several young men lifted up a twelve-foot-high cross, as tens of thousands of other youths lifted smaller ones. "It was an eerie, shattering scene," a reporter wrote, "as the street lights cast shadows on the young faces and the crosses held above them." At that moment, "a single word" from the pope could have started a riot or some effort to bring down the government. But John Paul simply said, "It's late, my friends. Let's go home quietly." He knew that these young people had years of sacrifice yet before them. The group began to disperse. As the papal limousine drove past, "the guitars played a farewell song." In the backseat of the car, the pope "covered his face in his hands and wept."

The last day of the pope's visit was June 10. In his final event that afternoon, the pope spoke during a closing Mass on the Blonia Krakowskie (the Krakow Commons), a 120-acre meadow inside the city limits of Krakow, the city in which he had spent most of his adult life. Before him was a crowd of between two and three million people. It was the largest gathering in Polish history. Weaving together his themes of man as a free actor and the centrality of the Church's role in Polish history, he again invoked Stanislaw, who "in the spiritual history of the Polish people" was a "patron of the Christian moral order. This order consists of a large number of tests, each one a test of faith and character. From every victorious test the moral order is built up. From every failed test moral disorder grows."

John Paul knew full well the severity of the tests that remained before the people who stood before him that day. Now his words to this massive gathering were intimate, even tender. He said:

> You must be strong, dear brothers and sisters. You must be strong with the strength that comes from faith. You must be faithful. Today more than in any other age you need this strength. You must be strong with the strength of hope, hope that brings the perfect joy of life and that does not allow us to grieve the Holy Spirit.
>
> You must be strong with love, which is stronger than death. You must be strong with the love that "is patient and kind; . . . is not jealous or boastful; . . . is not arrogant or rude . . . does not insist on its own way; . . . is not irritable or resentful; . . . does not rejoice at wrong, but rejoices in the right . . . bears all things, believes all things, hopes all things, endures all things. Love never ends." (1 Cor 13:4–8)

At last he began to say good-bye to the Polish people and to Poland—to which he did not know when he might return. "And so, before I leave you, I wish to give one more look at Krakow, this Krakow in which every stone and every brick is dear to me. And I look once more on my Poland."

His last words to them were a supplication, to embrace their true nature as human beings and as Poles:

> So, before going away, I beg you once more to accept the whole
>   of the spiritual legacy that goes by the name of "Poland" . . .
>   I beg you
> —never lose your trust, do not be defeated, do not be
>   discouraged;
> —do not on your own cut yourself off from the roots from which
>   we had our origins.
>   I beg you

—have trust notwithstanding all your weakness, always seek
spiritual power from him above from whom countless genera-
tions of our fathers and mothers have found it.

—never detach yourself from him.

—never lose your spiritual freedom, with which "he makes a
human being free."

—do not disdain charity, which is "the greatest of these" and
which shows itself through the Cross. Without it human life
has no roots and no meaning.

All this I beg of you . . .

—in the memory of St. Stanislaw who fell beneath the royal
sword at Skalka.

—all this I beg of you.

Amen.

Before going to the airport, the pope spoke briefly with journal-
ists who had covered his visit. Holding back tears, his voice
trembling, he said, "I hope, I hope, I hope to meet you again in
this country. I hope . . ." At the airport he brushed away tears
while standing on the tarmac, kissed the ground once more, and
then boarded the plane to Rome.

He left behind a nation of people with awakened consciences
and a renewed sense of personal dignity. He had told them, "The
future of Poland will depend on how many people are mature
enough to be nonconformist." By maturity he meant dignity; and
now they had the dignity, and the moral courage, not to conform
to the falsehoods of communist rule. Years of struggle still lay
before them. But in less than a decade, the seeds of their sacrifice
would bring freedom to Poles and tens of millions of people around
them. Wojtyla's visit was a triumph—the triumph of the principles
he had sketched out in solitude at a small desk not far from where
he stood that afternoon.

Embracing Solitude

Solitude has been instrumental to the effectiveness of leaders throughout history, but now they (along with everyone else) are losing it with hardly any awareness of the fact. Before the Information Age—which one could also call the Input Age— leaders naturally found solitude anytime they were physically alone, or when walking from one place to another, or while standing in line. Like a great wave that saturates everything in its path, however, handheld devices deliver immeasurable quantities of information and entertainment that now have virtually everyone instead staring down at their phones. Society did not make a considered choice to surrender the bulk of its time for reflection in favor of time spent reading tweets or texts.

Yet, with an awareness of what we have lost, each of us can choose to reclaim it. And leaders in particular—whose actions by definition affect not only themselves—have more than a choice. They have an obligation. A leader has not only permission, but a responsibility, to seek out periods of solitude. What follows are some ways to find it, and then use it productively.

Creating solitude at work

A leader must strike a balance between solitude and interaction with others, but leaders (along with everyone else) face considerable social pressure to skew the balance toward interaction. The term "loner" is usually a pejorative, often directed at people who spend only a fraction of their time alone. And in many offices the culture is to gather in herds—not only in meetings but at cake parties, lunch, and various events outside work. Some of these gatherings are worthwhile: if an event allows for meaningful interaction with your followers—to sound out how their work is progressing, if their needs are being met, and otherwise to hear what is happening in their lives—the leadership benefits of attendance likely outweigh the costs. But events comprising birthday cake and banter usually fail that test.

This same culture also finds physical manifestation, in open-office plans and large rooms full of cubicles. Here are some ways to overcome these obstacles, cultural and physical.

Reset expectations—expressly. Subordinates are entitled to clarity about not only what a leader expects of them, but what they can expect of their leader. A leader's accessibility is no exception. The assumption, unless the leader says otherwise, is that she is constantly accessible—if not in person, then electronically. But the task of changing that assumption requires only an act of will. A leader can designate a certain number of workdays per month as no-meeting days, as Nate Fick does. A leader can mark off sixty or ninety minutes on his calendar each day for time to think. A leader can make it known that he does not text, and checks his e-mail only intermittently or at certain points in the day. (One really has to wonder what leaders who make a point of responding to e-mails within minutes are otherwise doing with their time.) A leader can designate weekends as periods for no work-related e-mails to be sent at all, as Wendy Kopp has done at Teach for America. Or better yet, a leader can do all these things.

There is of course a certain price to be paid for changes like these. E-mails will go unanswered for hours rather than minutes, subordinates might have to wait sixty minutes to speak to a leader rather than do so immediately, and meetings about whatever the office tends to meet about might get pushed back a day. So be it. Scheduling a leader's time is a zero-sum game, and fundamentally what a leader must decide is whether reflection and hard analytical work are important enough to warrant perhaps a third of the leader's time, or whether instead those things deserve none of it.

There is another price for changes like these, namely the usual social levy upon nonconformity. Left unexplained, these changes will lead others to say the leader is arrogant, aloof, unapproachable. But there is no reason to leave the reasons for solitude unexplained. The leader can simply make clear, in as much or as little detail as she sees fit, that doing the organization's work requires time to think. And she can bear out that explanation during the times when she is accessible—by providing subordinates with clear comments upon their work rather than vague ones, thoughtful answers rather than platitudes, and otherwise performing like a leader who has thought through her guiding principles rather than made them up on the fly.

A leader who conspicuously marks off zones of solitude does not benefit herself alone. She also benefits her subordinates, by signaling that they have permission to do the same, for the same good reasons. The leader who sets aside time for solitude thereby creates a virtuous loop, to the betterment of everyone's work and the organization as a whole.

Find space for solitude. This task is admittedly difficult for anyone without an office door, yet there are ways to do it. If you do have an office door, have the courage to close it when you have reason to; that's what the door is for. If your workplace has a library, find reasons to go there; like a medieval church, its walls protect a culture often absent outside. An empty conference room could also serve, particularly if you spread lots of papers across the table. Both of these places, moreover, get you away from your computer and all the distractions that go with it. Lunchtime is also an occasion to seek time alone; if there are places where you can eat lunch outside—a park bench, a fountain square, almost anywhere that has a place to sit—go to them. They jog your thoughts out of the usual ruts. Eating alone in a restaurant is fine too; bring along some documents if you are worried about looking foolish. But leave your phone behind.

Solitude outside work

There are innumerable ways to find solitude outside work. Choosing among them depends on what you enjoy and what you're looking to accomplish. For analytical thinking or intuition, any activity that does not itself require focused attention will do: walking, running, early-morning rituals. One can also think with remarkable clarity while lying in bed in the minutes after awakening. Alternatively, one can engage in an activity that itself drives analysis, like journaling or memos to self. Other activities help clear out one's mind (which is the same kind of quietude one has upon awakening): meditation and Peter Crawford's night runs ("just focusing on my gait") are examples.

Physical exercise also releases nervous energy, and can thereby help to restore emotional balance. The same is true of meditation. Heading outdoors to hike or sit on a rock can restore perspective and cut one's problems down to size. To release excess emotion, one can also go to an empty room, or write a letter to a person one is upset with—and then not send it. And of course the outdoors can provide spiritual inspiration in countless ways. One can also find the same inspiration while sitting in an empty church.

And remember that solitude need not be an elaborate or drawn-out affair. Productive solitude is found as easily in the interstices of life as in its wide-open spaces. Driving on a highway, sitting in a waiting room, and dressing for work are all opportune times to think.

To obtain solitude outside work, one needs only to seek it.

Preparing for solitude

There are some simple ways to make solitude more productive. And there are reassurances to offer persons not accustomed to it.

Percolate beforehand. If you plan to use solitude to think about a specific issue, you should identify that issue in advance and briefly review any materials you think especially relevant. That will get your mind processing the issue beforehand, which often allows insights—sometimes analytical, sometimes intuitive—to come more quickly when you do think about it. Then you can spend your time in solitude thinking productively, rather than wasting time figuring out what, exactly, you should be thinking about. Moreover, if you're doing analytical thinking and are not making progress, turn to something else and then circle back with a more open, intuitive approach later. Frequently you'll find that your original analysis treated the issue as more complex than it actually is.

Prepare emotionally. Solitude routinely yields insights a leader does not expect, which is one of the principal reasons for seeking it. Even when a leader is thinking about some issue involving a subordinate or the organization as a whole, however, those insights are often about the leader himself: the realization that his own actions contributed to an employee's mistake, or that he has been focused only on his own problems, or that he has neglected some area of responsibility. Solitude brings one closer to the truth, and sometimes the truth is discomfiting. For a leader who is already humble, these insights are not devastating. And for any leader, they are opportunities to improve. Embrace them.

Extroverts will be fine. Extroverts gain energy from interaction with others, while introverts lose it. And introverts gain energy from solitude, while extroverts lose it. (For a definitive explanation of the differences between introverts and extroverts, see Susan Cain's *Quiet.*) But these energy transfers have little to do with how extroverts and introverts actually perform in these settings. Introverts can excel in social settings; extroverts can excel at thinking alone. The limitation is simply that members of each group can spend only so much time out of their element before they need to recharge.

That said, extroverts are not naturally drawn to solitude, nor is it typically part of their routine. Yet extroverts have as much to gain from solitude as anyone else. Admittedly, solitude can be lonely for extroverts at first. They enjoy talking about issues more than they do thinking about them alone. But extroverts will find that, when they identify the critical variables of a complex issue in advance, they enjoy talking about that issue even more. The energy they lose in solitude, they regain in a conversation that makes real progress on solving a problem they need to solve. Indeed extroverts will find that, when they make insights in solitude, the insights themselves will energize them. They will appreciate solitude even more as they experience its other benefits: creativity, emotional balance, and moral courage. And as shown by the profiles of extroverts in this book—Dwight Eisenhower and Bill George, both very strong extroverts, to name only two—extroverts will come to rely on solitude, indeed to treasure it, as they experience these benefits over time.

Don't worry about missing out. In some quarters there is a "fear of missing out": a fear that, if one unplugs from e-mail or news services or social media even for a few hours, they'll be less current (a few hours less, to be exact) than their peers. And indeed that is true. But tracking all these inputs is surrender to the Lilliputians. One simply cannot engage in anything more than superficial thought when cycling back and forth between these tweets and work. And most of the inputs are piecemeal, and thus worthless anyway. As with our obsession with smartphones, one needs to make a choice about whether to engage in this kind of practice. And no one serious about his responsibilities will choose to engage in it.

What to focus on in solitude

Our recommendations are threefold.

Embrace hard thinking. Even during time alone, it is easy for a leader to fool himself and everyone else into believing that he is doing substantive work when in fact he is merely reviewing superficial correspondence or performing functions that are almost ministerial. A leader should use solitude to identify his highest-value functions and then to do them. Among the most valuable functions a leader can perform is hard thinking about complex problems: identifying the problem precisely, making the premises of his thought explicit, and then examining each link in his logical chain—ideally all done on a notepad. There are fewer distractions that way.

Sometimes complex problems concern the organization as a whole. A leader who has not thought hard about those problems will favor off-the-rack solutions that are the leadership equivalent of the latest diet fad. Or the leader will offer only vague guidance to subordinates—"reassess this from a different angle," or "this needs to be buttoned up more"—because the leader himself lacks a clear idea of what he is looking for. A leader who embraces hard thinking can lead himself, and then others, through the process of finding effective solutions.

Other problems arise from the complex dynamics of interpersonal relationships. Solitude allows a leader to think carefully about what a particular subordinate needs, what that person might be worried about, or where the leader himself has fallen short in their relationship. A leader who reflects on his subordinates' well-being will enhance their effectiveness and earn their loyalty.

Identify your first principles and stay connected with them. A leader's first principles are the wellspring of all the benefits that solitude provides: clarity, creativity, emotional balance, and moral courage. A leader out of touch with his first principles will eventually run short of all these things. With a lack of direction internally, he will become directed externally. He will find himself governed by optics. He will have an uneasy awareness of a gap between what he thinks he believes and what he in fact chooses to do. The gap itself will reveal a lack of clarity in his thinking. And when others see the gap—when they say he is phony or hypocritical, and discount his leadership accordingly—he will have nothing to draw upon inside.

An authentic leader finds herself on different ground altogether. A leader who identifies her first principles and then periodically measures her actions against them is likely to act in accordance with them. That kind of leadership is inner-directed; and an inner-directed leader is unlikely to be diverted by moral criticism or praise. That is not to say a leader should be closed-minded: an effective leader will consider criticism on its merits, and when the critics have a point, she will act upon it. For the leader who has reflected deeply on her first principles, however, the criticism or praise that ultimately matters most is her own.

It is only this kind of leader—clear, balanced, courageous—who truly leads.

Find a higher purpose for your leadership, and share it with your followers. The most inspiring leaders are ones who find some transcendent meaning in the enterprise they lead. That meaning might spring from shared first principles, as it could for any organization that shares them in earnest. It might spring from a sense of shared injustice, or the realization that suffering confers dignity, or an awareness that honest labor does as well. Or it might spring from the devotion that a group's members share for one another. A transcendent meaning is one that by definition stands apart from the specific goals at hand. To find it, therefore, usually requires reflection.

The leaders who do find it are the ones we honor most.

Acknowledgments

Our thanks go first to George Gibson, Bloomsbury's publisher and the editor of this book, whose insights and suggestions, large and small, made this a much better book than it otherwise would have been. George is decent, generous, and erudite; and we have been privileged, both professionally and personally, to have worked with him. Also at Bloomsbury, we thank Derek Stordahl, for giving us a chance and for connecting us with George; Jenna Dutton, for her patience and effort in leading the book to production; and India Cooper, for her thoughtful suggestions and for saving us from our own mistakes. Bloomsbury truly does treat its authors extraordinarily well.

We are grateful to Jim Collins, who has been a superb mentor to Mike, and whose foreword captures the essence of this book. Jim's focus on improving leadership from "good to great" inspired us to write about how great leaders throughout history have used solitude to be more effective. And otherwise Jim's support and encouragement were instrumental in making this book a reality.

We also thank Larry Olson, who is as generous a friend as one could ever hope for. For six years, as we worked on this project, Larry encouraged and guided us and gave us the benefit of his expertise in the publishing business. This book would not have happened without Larry, and we are deeply grateful to him.

We are likewise grateful to Susan and Ken Cain, who were

extremely generous with their time and advice, and whose encouragement sustained us during our wilderness years of working on this project. We are more indebted to them than we can say.

We owe a debt of inspiration to Bill Deresiewicz, the accomplished author and former Yale professor. Bill's 2009 speech at West Point—entitled "Solitude and Leadership," and later published by the *American Scholar* online, where it went viral— sparked a conversation between Mike and Ray one spring day at an Irish pub in Ann Arbor, which in turn led us to pursue the idea of this book. We are only two of many thousands of people inspired by Bill's work.

This book would not have been possible without the generosity and candor of the people who agreed to be interviewed and then profiled in it: Jimmy Bartz, Dena Braeger, Dan Brostek, Brené Brown, Tommy Caldwell, Doug Conant, Peter Crawford, Sarah Dillard, Chip Edens, Nate Fick, Bill George, Tim Hall, Liza Howard, General (Retired) James Mattis, General (Retired) Stanley McChrystal, General (Retired) Montgomery Meigs, General (Retired) Howard Prince, Joey Reiman, Sanyin Siang, Katie Simonis, Pam Slim, and Jaya Vadlamudi. We are also grateful to the many other people who described for us, often in writing, the ways in which they have used solitude to be more effective as leaders: Jonathan Algor, Nick Armstrong, Dominic Barton, Jeff Bryan, Mike Cooper, Ryan Friedrichs, John Green, Dan Horst, Scott Barry Kaufman, Wendy Kopp, Jay McGee, Joe Quinn, Condoleezza Rice, John Ryan, Rajiv Srinivasan, Glenn Thomas, Casey Thoreen, Tom Tierney, and Kathy White.

We also wish to thank Ray's former law clerk Charles Dameron and his wife Emily Esfahani Smith, who are both accomplished writers (Emily recently authored *The Power of Meaning*), and who both provided wise advice about the structure and content of this book. We likewise thank Ray's former law clerk Phillip Williamson, whose suggestions during a car ride from Ann Arbor to Cincinnati one day greatly improved the chapter on Martin Luther King Jr. Our thanks also go to Marcia Carter for her support as we wrote the book. And we thank the University of Michigan's Hatcher

Graduate Library, where Ray studied in the stacks as an under-graduate, and whose magnificent collection of books (seemingly almost every book ever published) was invaluable to us in research-ing and writing this book.

Two people deserve our special thanks: Ray's former law clerk James "J.J." Snidow and Ray's dad, Raymond A. Ketchledge. (The variation in the spelling of Ray's surname and his dad's is a long story.) For years, each of them read every word of this book as it was written; and each of them told us to stay the course when we were right, and (often in no uncertain terms, especially in the case of Ray's dad) to change course when we were wrong. Their judg-ment seemed always to coincide, and we came to trust it completely. J.J. is a born leader and gifted writer, and offered superb editorial suggestions along with the perspective of his generation. Ray's dad tested everything we wrote against his long experience as a senior executive in the car business, and offered substantive insights too numerous to count. Ray's dad also gave us the signal advice to "protect your vision of the book." We are deeply indebted to them both.

Finally, we thank Ray's daughter, Ella, who loves animals and reading, and who suggested that we profile Jane Goodall as a leader in this book. And we thank Ray's wife, Jessica, and Mike's wife, Genevieve, whose love and support sustained each of us throughout.

Notes

Chapter 1: Clarity

PAGE 4:   **"a process of assigning"** *United States v. Gabrion*, 719 F.3d 511, 533 (6th Cir. 2013).

All Bill George quotations are from the authors' interview, May 11, 2015. For a short primer on transcendental meditation, see Yogani, *Deep Meditation* (Nashville: AYP Publishing, 2005). For a summary of medical research concerning meditation, see Norman E. Rosenthal, M.D., *Transcendence* (New York: Penguin, 2011).

All Peter Crawford quotations are from the authors' interview, March 29, 2016.

All Liza Howard quotations are from the authors' interview, March 23, 2016.

The quotation from General James Mattis is from the authors' interview, February 10, 2011.

All Sarah Dillard quotations are from the authors' interview, March 22, 2016.

All Nate Fick quotations are from the authors' interview, March 3, 2011.

All the quotations from General Stanley McChrystal are from the authors' interview, June 23, 2016.

All General Howard Prince quotations are from the authors' interviews, February 18, 2011, and March 22, 2016.

All Susan Cain quotations are from the authors' interview, April 5, 2016.

All Tommy Caldwell quotations are from the authors' interview, January 29, 2016.

Chapter 2: Analytical Clarity

PAGE 27:   **"What should be" "a curious echo" "Marshall—he is close"** Dwight D. Eisenhower, *Crusade in Europe* (Baltimore: Johns Hopkins University Press, 1997), 18.

PAGE 28:   **"I agree"** Stephen Ambrose, *The Supreme Commander* (New York: Anchor Books, 2012), 6: Eisenhower, *Crusade*, 22.

PAGE 28:   **"throughout his life"** John S. D. Eisenhower, ed., *Letters to Mamie* (Garden City, NY: Doubleday, 1978), 7.

PAGE 29:   **"the strain comes from"** Ibid., 94–95.

PAGE 29:   **"Talk-talk-talk"** Alfred D. Chandler, ed., *The Papers of Dwight David Eisenhower, The War Years*, 5 vols. (Baltimore: Johns Hopkins University Press, 1970), 1:35.

PAGE 29:   **"This is the longest stretch"** Eisenhower, *Letters to Mamie*, 46–47.

PAGE 29:   **"My days are always"** Ibid., 173.

PAGE 29:   **"My hours in the office"** Ibid., 178.

PAGE 29:   **"When I get driven"** Ibid., 130.

PAGE 29:   **"the far-reaching . . . Russian collapse"** Robert H. Ferrell, ed., *The Eisenhower Diaries* (New York: Norton, 1981), 417–418.

PAGE 30:   **"An orderly, logical mind"** Ibid., 87.

PAGE 30:   **"To crystallize"** Chandler, *Papers of Eisenhower, The War Years* 2:844.

PAGE 30:   **"How in hell"** Ibid., 1:83.

PAGE 30:   **"We must get going!"** Ibid., 328.

PAGE 30:   **rat-infested catacomb** Rick Atkinson, *An Army at Dawn* (New York: Henry Holt, 2002), 59.

PAGE 31:   **wrote out on a sheet** Ibid., 115.

PAGE 31:   **"We cannot find"** Chandler, *Papers of Eisenhower* 2:675.

PAGE 31:   **"clarify his thoughts"** Ibid., 910.

PAGE 31:   **"the newspapers want"** Ibid., 778.

PAGE 31:   **"terribly sad"** Eisenhower, *Letters to Mamie*, 175.

PAGE 31–32:   **"There was no" "used the occasion"** Carlo D'Este, *Eisenhower: A Soldier's Life* (New York: Henry Holt, 2002), 393.

PAGE 32:   **"As I approached"** Ibid., 417.

PAGE 32:   **"inner peace"** Ibid, 418.

PAGE 32:   **"Ike is deeply concerned"** Ibid., 440.

PAGE 32:   **"I must so seriously"** Chandler, *Papers of Eisenhower* 2:1340.

PAGE 33:   **"General Patton continues"** Ibid., 1353.

PAGE 33:   **"since it seems to be"** Ibid., 3:1837.

PAGE 33:   **"General Patton has progressed" "the face of every one"** D'Este, *Life*, 506.

PAGE 33:   **"I'm just about"** Ibid., 507.

PAGE 33:   **"I fully concurred"** Ibid., 509.

PAGE 33–34:   **"can do a very fine"** Chandler, *Papers of Eisenhower* 3:1840–41.

PAGE 34:   **"I must tell you frankly"** Ibid., 1839–40.

PAGE 34–35:   **"you carry the burden" "like you I have"** Ibid., 1838.

PAGE 35:   **"The decision is"** Ibid., 1841.

PAGE 35:   **"I am once more"** D'Este, *Life*, 508-09.

PAGE 35–36:   **"In early December . . . considering the problem"** Ibid., 1711–12.

PAGE 36:   **"the only remaining"** Eisenhower, *Crusade*, 245.

PAGE 36:   **"futile slaughter"** Ambrose, *Supreme Commander*, 407.

PAGE 36:   **"it would be difficult"** Eisenhower, *Crusade*, 245.

PAGE 37:   **"I went to my tent"** Ibid., 246.

PAGE 38:   **"a great human spring"** Ibid., 249.

PAGE 38:   **"one of Eisenhower's characteristics"** Ambrose, *Supreme Commander*, 251.

PAGE 38:   **"We must go"** Chandler, *Papers of Eisenhower* 3:1905.

PAGE 38:   **"scientist to his bones"** D'Este, *Life*, 523.

PAGE 39:   **rattled the windowpanes . . . "I am quite positive"** Ambrose, *Supreme Commander*, 415.

PAGE 40:   **sank into a sofa** D'Este, *Life*, 525.

PAGE 40:   **"Okay, let's go"** Ambrose, *Supreme Commander*, 417.

PAGE 40:   **"Our landings in"** Ibid., 418.

PAGE 40:   **"Well, it's on"** Ibid., 419.

Chapter 3: The Stillness of Intuition

PAGE 42:   **"from many specific"** Bryan Garner, *Garner's Modern American Usage*, 3rd ed. (Oxford: Oxford University Press, 2009), 231.

PAGE 44:   **"Behavior does not"** Goodall and Berman, *Reason for Hope*, 53.

PAGE 45:   **"could not bear"** Jane Goodall, *In the Shadow of Man* (Boston: Mariner, 2000), 25.

PAGE 46:   **"following each other" "marked the turning point"** Ibid., 26.

PAGE 46:   **"As soon as I was sure"** Ibid., 32.

PAGE 46–47:   **Mr. McGregor** Ibid., 32.

PAGE 47:   **Flo** Ibid., 32, 79.

PAGE 47:   **"had a relaxed"** Jane Goodall, *Through a Window* (Boston: Houghton Mifflin, 1990), 33.

PAGE 47:   **"it was impossible"** Goodall, *In the Shadow of Man*, 83.

PAGE 47:   **"was a highly competent"** Goodall, *Through a Window*, 33.

PAGE 47:   **"At once Flo sprang"** Ibid., 30.

PAGE 47:   **Passion** Ibid, 33.

PAGE 47:   **snatch the infant away** Ibid., 77–78.

PAGE 47:   **"calm and unafraid"** Goodall, *Through a Window*, 240.

PAGE 48:   **"He gave my offering"** Dale Peterson, ed., *Africa in My Blood* (Boston: Houghton Mifflin, 2000), 267.

PAGE 48:   **"had no idea"** Goodall, *Through a Window*, 14.

PAGE 48:   **escorts had left her** Dale Peterson, *Jane Goodall* (Boston: Houghton Mifflin, 2006), 230.

PAGE 48:   **"a period I remember"** Goodall, *In the Shadow of Man*, 30.

PAGE 49:   **"getting closer to animals"** Goodall and Berman, *Reason for Hope*, 72.

PAGE 49:   **"The feel of rough"** Peterson, *Jane Goodall*, 234; Goodall and Berman, *Reason for Hope*, 73.

PAGE 49:   **"Words are part"** Ibid., 79.

PAGE 49:   **"No words of mine"** Goodall, *In the Shadow of Man*, 30.

PAGE 49:   **"The air was filled"** Goodall, *Through a Window*, 10–11.

PAGE 49:   **not set apart from** Ibid., 207; Goodall and Berman, *Hope*, 81.

PAGE 50:   **guided her intuition** Goodall, *Through a Window*, 17; Goodall and Berman, *Reason for Hope*, 77.

Chapter 4: Creativity

PAGE 53:   **Becquerel's discovery . . . darkened the plates** Robert Reid, *Marie Curie* (New York: Collins, 1974), 78-79.

PAGE 54:   **amount of energy . . . uranium atom itself** Ibid., 81.

All Joey Reiman quotations are from the authors' interviews, May 24, 2011, and February 22, 2016.

All Dena Braeger quotations are from the authors' interview, May 9, 2016.

All Tim Hall quotations are from the authors' interview, March 21, 2016.

All General Montgomery Meigs quotations are from his written submission to the authors, June 2011.

All Chip Edens quotations are from the authors' interviews, January 27 and 28, 2016.

Chapter 5: "Suppose We Were a Thing Intangible"

PAGE 69:   **Winston Churchill grasped** Carlos D'Este, *Warlord* (New York: HarperCollins, 2008), 217–22.

PAGE 69:   **"in all my life" "So the duty"** T.E. Lawrence, *Seven Pillars of Wisdom* (New York: Doubleday, 1935), 114.

PAGE 69:   **"A weariness of the desert"** Ibid., 157.

PAGE 71:   **"I have never seen"** John E. Mack, *A Prince of Our Disorder* (Boston: Little, Brown, 1976), 295–96.

PAGE 71:   **"At moments of thought"** Ibid., 296.

PAGE 71–72:   **"which, with an" "not intellect" "master-spirit" "affected openness"** Lawrence, *Seven Pillars*, 67.

PAGE 72:   **"lad of nineteen"** Ibid., 77.

PAGE 72:   **"dignified and admirable" "without great force"** Ibid., 76.

PAGE 72:   **"very tall and pillar-like"** Ibid., 97.

PAGE 72:   **"showed a mastery of tact"** Ibid. 98.

PAGE 72:   **"seemed to govern"** Ibid.

PAGE 73:   **"suitable maxims"** Ibid., 188.

PAGE 73:   **"the aim of war"** Ibid., 189.

PAGE 73:   **"was geographical"** Ibid, 191.

PAGE 73:   **"did not fit"** Ibid., 188.

PAGE 73:   **"alternative end"** Ibid, 190.

PAGE 73:   **"it dawned on me"** Ibid., 189.

PAGE 73–74:   **"how would the Turks" "by a trench line" "Suppose we were"** Ibid., 192.

PAGE 74:   **"space was greater"** Ibid., 196.

PAGE 74:   **"develop a habit" "In railway-cutting"** Ibid., 194.

PAGE 74:   **"need a fortified"** Ibid., 192.

PAGE 74:   **"Final victory"** Ibid., 196.

PAGE 75:   **"within gunfire" "was so entirely"** Ibid., 225.

PAGE 75:   **"'Auda is here'"** Ibid., 221.

PAGE 75:   **"He must be nearly" "Turks are not counted"** Malcolm Brown, ed., *T.E. Lawrence in War and Peace* (London: Greenhill Books, 2005), 132–33.

PAGE 75–75:   **"since two bullets"** Ibid., 139.

Chapter 6: Emotional Balance

PAGE 79:   **"The rebel army"** Shelby Foote, *The Civil War*, vol. 2 (New York: Random House, 1963), 281.

All General James Mattis quotations are from the authors' interview, February 10, 2011.

All Jaya Vadlamudi quotations are from the authors' interview, May 7, 2016.

All Katy Simonis quotations are from the authors' interview, March 22, 2016.

All Pam Slim quotations are from the authors' interview, March 7, 2016.

All Sanyin Siang quotations are from the authors' interview, March 14, 2016.

Chapter 7: Acceptance

PAGE 99: **"possessed extraordinary empathy"** Doris Kearns Goodwin, *Team of Rivals* (New York: Simon & Schuster, 2005), 104.

PAGE 99: **"Our task is not"** James M. McPherson, *Tried by War: Abraham Lincoln as Commander in Chief* (New York: Penguin, 2008), 182.

PAGE 100: **"Will our Generals"** Michael Burlingame and John R. Turner Ettlinger, eds., *Inside Lincoln's White House: The Complete Civil War Diary of John Hay* (Carbondale: Southern Illinois University Press, 1997), 62.

PAGE 100: **"the literal or substantial"** McPherson, *Tried by War*, 183.

PAGE 100: **mud, his men's exhaustion, and the strength** Ibid., 183

PAGE 100: **"walked up and down"** Burlingame and Ettlinger, *Inside Lincoln's White House*, 302–03.

PAGE 100: **"You will follow up"** Ibid., 304.

PAGE 100: **"the President seemed"** Ibid., 61.

PAGE 100: **"the Prest was"** Ibid., 62.

PAGE 100: **"grief and anger"** Ibid., 303.

PAGE 100–101: **"What does it" "On only one" "was more grieved"** McPherson, *Tried by War*, 184.

PAGE 101: **"The Tycoon"** Burlingame and Ettlinger, *Inside Lincoln's White House*, 64.

PAGE 101: **"in tears"** Carl Sandburg, *Abraham Lincoln: The Prairie Years and the War Years* (New York: Harcourt, Brace, 1954), 415.

PAGE 101–102: **"I am very . . . because of it"** Roy P. Basler, ed., *Abraham Lincoln: His Speeches and Writings* (Cleveland: World, 1946), 711.

PAGE 102: **"never sent"** Ibid., 712.

PAGE 102: **"Lincoln's ability"** Goodwin, *Team of Rivals*, 609.

PAGE 104: **"I am profoundly grateful"** Sandburg, *Abraham Lincoln*, 415; McPherson, *Tried by War*, 186.

PAGE 104: **"I have rarely seen"** Michael Burlingame, ed., *At Lincoln's Side: John Hay's Civil War Correspondence and Selected Writings* (Carbondale: Southern Illinois Univ. Press 2006), 49.

Chapter 8: Cartharsis

PAGE 106: **"confines himself to" "a man who could"** Shelby Foote, *The Civil War*, vol. 2 (New York: Random House, 1963), 218.

PAGE 106: **"Grant was calmer"** Jean Edward Smith, *Grant* (New York: Simon & Schuster, 2001), 295.

PAGE 106–107: **"Here was no"** Foote, *Civil War* 2:219.

PAGE 107:   **Grant was no-nonsense "as plain as"** Smith, *Grant*, 233.

PAGE 107:   **"I say, stranger"** Ibid., 333.

PAGE 107:   **"remembered the most" "and in fact"** Ibid., 233.

PAGE 107:   **"in battle, the sphinx"** Ibid., 295.

PAGE 108:   **"withdrawn behind a barrier" "General, this won't"** Foote, *Civil War* 2:219.

PAGE 108:   **"could give him a dozen"** Ibid., 220.

PAGE 109:   **"the whole thing" "I tremble"** Ibid., 332.

PAGE 109:   **"we give up"** Ibid., 324.

PAGE 109–110: **"I think our troops"** Ibid., 323.

PAGE 111:   **"a sense of"** Shelby Foote, *The Civil War*, vol. 3 (New York: Random House, 1974), 149–50.

PAGE 111:   **"if any opportunity"** Ibid., 3:158.

PAGE 112:   **"Grant calmly took"** Smith, *Grant*, 320.

PAGE 112:   **"Grant took a seat"** Foote, *Civil War* 3:159.

PAGE 112–113: **"General Grant by"** Horace Porter, *Campaigning with Grant* (Lincoln: University of Nebraska Press, 2000), 52.

PAGE 113:   **"sat for a time"** Smith, *Grant*, 323–24.

PAGE 113:   **"we are driving"** Ibid., 326.

PAGE 113:   **"overcome with emotion"** Ibid, 327.

PAGE 113:   **"off his balance"** Ibid., 328.

PAGE 113:   **staff in turmoil** Ibid., 329.

PAGE 113:   **"his orders calmly"** Foote, *Civil War* 3:184.

PAGE 113–114: **"never exhibited" "It strikes me"** Smith, *Grant*, 329.

PAGE 114:   **"our lines broke"** Ibid., 330.

PAGE 115:   **"This is a crisis" "Oh, I am heartily" "the coming of" "without uttering any word" "with a degree of"** Foote, *Civil War* 3:185.

PAGE 116:   **"Grant went into"** Ibid., 185–86.

PAGE 116:   **"never before seen"** Ibid., 186.

PAGE 116:   **"We had waged"** Sylvanus Cadwallader, *Three Years With Grant* (Lincoln: University of Nebraska Press, 1955), 180–81.

PAGE 117:   **"For minutes that" "I happened to look" "commenced a pleasant"** Ibid., 181.

PAGE 117:   **"smilingly assented"** Ibid, 181–82.

PAGE 117:   **"It was the grandest"** Ibid., 182.

PAGE 117:   **"Our spirits rose"** Foote, *Civil War* 3:191.

Chapter 9: Magnanimity

PAGE 120:   **"I feel spiritually"** Gustaaf Houtman, *Mental Culture in Burmese Crisis Politics* (Tokyo: Institute for the Study of Languages and Cultures of Asia and Africa, 1999), 291.

PAGE 120: **"She put down"** Aung San Suu Kyi, *Freedom from Fear* (London: Penguin 1991), xv.

PAGE 121: **"I could not"** Peter Popham, *The Lady and the Peacock* (New York: The Experiment, 2011), 56.

PAGE 121: **the army repeatedly** Justin Wintle, *Perfect Hostage* (London: Hutchinson, 2007) 274, 75.

PAGE 121: **sent to Insein Jail** Popham, *Lady and the Peacock*, 245.

PAGE 121: **swept 392 of 485** Suu Kyi, *Freedom from Fear*, xxiv

PAGE 122: **"The first years"** Popham, *Lady and the Peacock*, 289.

PAGE 122: **refused to receive** Ibid., 290.

PAGE 122: **lacked telephone service** Ibid., 290-91; Wintle, *Hostage*, 346–47.

PAGE 122: **never tempted** Aung San Suu Kyi, *The Voice of Hope* (New York: Seven Stories, 2008), 145.

PAGE 122: **"'It's you and me'"** Popham, *Lady and the Peacock*, 290–91.

PAGE 122: **Each morning she** Wintle, *Perfect Hostage*, 347.

PAGE 123: **"I remember everything"** Suu Kyi, *The Voice of Hope*, 34.

PAGE 123: **to purify not only** Sayadaw U Pandita, *In This Very Life*, (Boston: Wisdom Publications, 1992), 11.

PAGE 123: **"*metta* wishes the welfare"** Ibid., 197.

PAGE 123: **"Engaged Buddhism"** Suu Kyi, *Voice of Hope*, 43.

PAGE 123: ***karunna*, or "active compassion"** Houtman, *Mental Culture in Burmese Crisis Politics, 193.*

PAGE 123: **"a breadth of vision"** Suu Kyi, *Voice of Hope*, 180.

PAGE 123: **"A lot of us"** Ibid., 166.

PAGE 124: **govern "on the basis"** Suu Kyi, *Freedom from Fear*, 191.

PAGE 124: **"revolution of the spirit"** Suu Kyi, *Voice of Hope*, 82.

PAGE 124: **"It is *metta*"** Popham, *Lady and the Peacock*, 312.

PAGE 124: **the Burmese regime refused** Ibid., 332–33.

PAGE 124: **killed 70** Ibid., 359.

PAGE 125: **"turn the page"** Ibid., 363.

PAGE 125: **"We were almost"** Ibid., 363–64.

PAGE 125: **The monks are** Ibid., 373.

PAGE 125: **"May all sentient beings"** Ibid., 376.

PAGE 126: **"as a menace"** Ibid., 399.

PAGE 126: **"against the will"** Ibid., 398.

PAGE 126: **"the real change"** Suu Kyi, *The Voice of Hope*, 181.

Chapter 10: Moral Courage

PAGE 129: **"looking at you like"** Jack Bass, *Taming the Storm* (New York: Doubleday, 1993), 356.

PAGE 129:   **principal target** Ibid., 124–25, 195.

PAGE 129:   **"nobody took his"** Ibid., 316.

PAGE 130:   **"believe in a"** Ibid., 364.

PAGE 130:   **"always measured by"** Ibid., 113.

PAGE 130:   **"sole duty"** Ibid., 164.

All Doug Conant quotations are from the authors' interview, March 14, 2016.

All Dena Braeger quotations are from the authors' interview, May 9, 2016.

All Dan Brostek quotations are from the authors' interview, February 5, 2016.

All Brené Brown quotations are from the authors' interview, July 29, 2016.

All Jimmy Bartz quotations are from the authors' interview, February 1, 2016.

PAGE 141:   **"It is by habituating"** Aristotle, *The Nicomachean Ethics* (New York: Penguin, 2004), 35.

Chapter 11: "A Sublime Power to Rise Above"

PAGE 143:   **"the warmest of welcomes"** William Manchester, *The Last Lion: Alone, 1932–1940* (Boston: Little, Brown, 1988), 359–60.

PAGE 143–144:   **"even the descriptions" "My good friends"** Ibid., 360.

PAGE 144:   **"For the moment"** Martin Gilbert, *The Churchill Documents*, vol. 13 (Hillsdale, MI: Hillsdale Press, 1982), 1180.

PAGE 144:   **"I will begin"** David Cannadine, ed. *Blood, Toil, Tears, and Sweat* (Boston: Houghton Mifflin, 1989), 130.

PAGE 145:   **"prepared to risk" "liberation"** Manchester, *Last Lion*, 338.

PAGE 145:   **"whether the Sudetens"** Robert C. Self, ed., *The Neville Chamberlain Diary Letters* (Burlington: Ashgate 2000), vol. 3, 348.

PAGE 145:   **"secure their approval"** Ibid., 339.

PAGE 146:   **"no longer possible"** Ibid., 340.

PAGE 146:   **bade the Fuhrer** Ibid, 340.

PAGE 147:   **less than 5 percent** Peter Clarke, *Mr. Churchill's Profession* (New York: Bloomsbury Press, 2012), 135.

PAGE 147:   **a total of nearly** Ibid., 241.

PAGE 147:   **"The quintessential Churchill"** Manchester, *Last Lion*, 304.

PAGE 148:   **"characteristic, elevating"** Clarke, *Mr. Churchill's Profession*, 213.

PAGE 148:   **"if the British Empire"** Cannadine, *Blood*, 178.

PAGE 148:   **"at the moment"** Gilbert, *Churchill Documents* 13:1123.

PAGE 148:   **"It has been"** Ibid., 1160.

PAGE 149:   **"And wherever men"** Winston S. Churchill, *A History of the English-Speaking Peoples*, vol. 1 (London: Cassell, 1956), 47.

PAGE 149:   **"I have just finished"** Gilbert, *Churchill Documents*, 13:1328.

PAGE 149:   **"There welled in the heart"** Churchill, *History*, 328.

PAGE 149:   **"Have we not"** Winston S. Churchill, *Blood Sweat and Tears*
                (New York: G. P. Putnam's Sons, 1941), 22.

PAGE 149:   **"in this ancient Forest"** Ibid., 49.

PAGE 149:   **"Whatever may happen"** Ibid., 51.

PAGE 150:   **"I venture to think"** Ibid., 135.

PAGE 150:   **"Czechoslovakia has ceased"** Manchester, *Last Lion*, 393.

PAGE 150:   **"Frequently, as he dictates"** Ibid., 32.

PAGE 150:   **"nothing can detract"** Chartwell Papers, Churchill College
                of Cambridge University, 9/130B/140.

PAGE 150:   **"All is over" "this particular block"** Cannadine, *Blood, Toil*,
                134–35.

PAGE 151:   **"I must say"** Ibid., 137.

PAGE 151:   **"A sublime power"** Churchill, *History* 1:92.

PAGE 151:   **"I do not grudge"** Cannadine, *Blood, Toil*, 143.

Chapter 12: "No Never Alone"

PAGE 154:   **"Leadership never ascends"** David J. Garrow, *Bearing the
                Cross* (New York: HarperCollins, 1986), 50.

PAGE 154:   **King declined, citing** Ibid., 51.

PAGE 155:   **"did not have to"** Ibid., 17–18.

PAGE 155:   **in cars driven by** Ibid., 21.

PAGE 155:   **"Well, if you think"** Ibid., 22.

PAGE 156:   **"You know something"** Taylor Branch, *Parting the Waters*
                (New York: Touchstone, 1988), 138.

PAGE 156:   **One thousand people** Garrow, *Bearing the Cross*, 23.

PAGE 156:   **"We are here . . . feet of oppression"** Clayborne Carson
                et al., eds., *The Papers of Martin Luther King, Jr.*, vol. 3
                (Berkeley: University of California, 1992), 71–72.

PAGE 156:   **"like a wave"** Branch, *Parting the Waters*, 138.

PAGE 156–157:   **"And we are not wrong . . . mighty stream"** Ibid., 140–41;
                Carson et al., *King Papers*, 3:74.

PAGE 157:   **"Let us think"** Ibid., 74.

PAGE 157:   **The crowd roared** Garrow, *Bearing the Cross*, 24.

PAGE 157:   **people reached out** Branch, *Parting the Waters*, 142.

PAGE 157:   **blacks were often** J. Mills Thornton III, *Dividing Lines*
                (Tuscaloosa: University of Alabama Press, 2002), 41–42.

PAGE 158:   **wherever they happened** Ibid., 45.

PAGE 158:   **"practically rubbing knees"** Branch, *Parting the Waters*, 146.

PAGE 158:   **"ministers of the gospel"** Ibid., 147.

PAGE 158:   **A similar system** Ibid., 146.
PAGE 159:   **"preconceived ideas . . . to my rescue"** Garrow, *Bearing the Cross*, 30–31.
PAGE 159:   **"a terrible sense"** Branch, *Parting*, 148.
PAGE 159:   **Parker was taken aback** Ibid., 148–49.
PAGE 159–160:   **"why the older" offered to resign** Garrow, *Bearing the Cross*, 51.
PAGE 160:   **received a standing** Branch, *Parting the Waters*, 150.
PAGE 160:   **"in effect, the Montgomery"** Garrow, *Cross*, 52.
PAGE 160:   **membership in the Montgomery White Citizens** Thornton, *Dividing Lines*, 73.
PAGE 160:   **strained to the limit** Branch, *Parting the Waters*, 150–51.
PAGE 161:   **"highfalutin preacher"** Ibid., 154.
PAGE 161:   **Montgomery police began** Ibid., 159.
PAGE 161:   **"Get out, King" about to be lynched** Ibid., 160.
PAGE 161:   **released King upon** Garrow, *Bearing the Cross*, 56.
PAGE 161:   **"It was the most"** Ibid., 57.
PAGE 162:   **"I felt myself faltering"** Ibid., 56.
PAGE 162:   **"We are tired"** Ibid., 57–58.
PAGE 162–163:   **"I started thinking . . . My uncertainty disappeared"** Ibid., 58.
PAGE 163:   **"an explosion"** Ibid., 59.
PAGE 163:   **"We are not advocating"** Ibid., 60.
PAGE 163–164:   **"accepted the word"** Ibid.
PAGE 164:   **segregation on the city's buses** Thornton, *Dividing Lines*, 90, 93.
PAGE 164:   **"So I'm not afraid"** Garrow, *Cross*, 89.
PAGE 165:   **"Well, I don't know"** Ibid., 621.

Chapter 13: The Dignity Not to Conform

PAGE 167:   **"every cross placed"** George Weigel, *Witness to Hope* (New York: HarperCollins, 1999), 310.
PAGE 167:   **His only sister . . . of his family** Ibid., 29–31.
PAGE 167–168:   **after attending mass . . . dive-bombers** George Weigel, *City of Saints* (New York: Image, 2015), 48–49.
PAGE 168:   **nine hundred calories a day** Weigel, *Witness to Hope*, 51, 55; Catherine Pepinster, *John Paul II: Reflections from the Tablet* (New York: Continuum, 2005), 67.
PAGE 168:   **temperatures as low as** Weigel, *Witness to Hope*, 56.
PAGE 168:   **"I never felt"** Ibid., 68.
PAGE 168:   **"that has not been climbed"** Kwitny, *Man of the Century*, 147.

PAGE 168:   **his face distant** Weigel, *Witness to Hope*, 103; Tad Szulc, *Pope John Paul II* (New York: Scribner, 1995), 181.

PAGE 169:   ***Wujek*** Kwitny, *Man of the Century*, 131.

PAGE 169:   **"switch off" ride into a tree** Ibid., 131

PAGE 169:   **"often took his"** Ibid., 191; Weigel, *Witness to Hope*, 188.

PAGE 169:   **"granite integrity"** Ibid., 30.

PAGE 169:   **also to its Jews** Ibid., 23–24.

PAGE 169:   **chose to play for** Szulc, *Pope John Paul II*, 68.

PAGE 169:   **Jerzy Kluger** Ibid., 283.

PAGE 169:   **"example was in"** Weigel, *Witness to Hope*, 31.

PAGE 169:   **they treated the young** Ibid., 56.

PAGE 170:   **"The whole greatness"** Weigel, *City of Saints*, 96.

PAGE 170:   **"their living situations"** Weigel, *Witness to Hope*, 57.

PAGE 170:   **no appointment required** Ibid., 201.

PAGE 170:   **an old green coat** Weigel, *City of Saints*, 193.

PAGE 170:   **give it away to** Weigel, *Witness to Hope*, 201.

PAGE 171:   **at age thirty-eight** George Weigel, *The End and the Beginning* (New York: Doubleday, 2010), 52.

PAGE 171:   ***defensor populi*** Weigel, *Witness to Hope*, 182.

PAGE 171:   **Archbishop Adam Stefan Sapieha** Ibid., 72–73.

PAGE 171:   **SB agents tailed** Weigel, *End and Beginning*, 58; Weigel, *City of Saints*, 172.

PAGE 171:   **by 1967 some 270** Weigel, *End and Beginning*, 60.

PAGE 171–172: **One memo, prepared** Ibid., 58–59.

PAGE 172:   **"Wojtyla is a very dangerous"** Ibid., 68.

PAGE 172:   **a small desk alone** Weigel, *Witness to Hope*, 188.

PAGE 172:   **"numerous philosophical essays"** Ibid., 210.

PAGE 172:   **"the true champion"** Weigel, *End and Beginning*, 88.

PAGE 172:   **"culture of the lie"** Ibid., 64.

PAGE 172:   **A Polish joke** Weigel, *Witness to Hope*, 133.

PAGE 172–173: **Wojtyla argued that** Weigel, *End and Beginning*, 47.

PAGE 173:   **"an integral part"** Weigel, *City of Saints*, 199.

PAGE 173:   **"*You* must decide"** Ibid., 201.

PAGE 173:   **Father Maximilian Kolbe** Weigel, *Witness to Hope*, 78, 314.

PAGE 174:   **"to visit the adjacent"** Weigel, *City of Saints*, 211.

PAGE 174:   **two million individual** Ibid., 214–15; Weigel, *Witness to Hope*, 190.

PAGE 175:   **"Tell the Pope"** Ibid., 301.

PAGE 175:   **"may have been"** Ibid., 295.

PAGE 175:   **"of Europe and"** John Paul II, *Return to Poland* (New York: Collins, 1979), 24–25.

PAGE 175–176: **"a son of ... capable of them"** John Paul II, *Return to Poland*, 25.

PAGE 176:   **"We want God"** Weigel, *Witness to Hope*, 293.

PAGE 176:   **"Christ cannot be . . . of the nation."** John Paul II, *Return to Poland*, 28–29.

PAGE 176:   **"We are before . . . Poland is made"** Ibid., 29.

PAGE 177:   **"by each son . . . on Victory Square"** Ibid., 29–30.

PAGE 177:   **"And I cry"** Ibid., 30.

PAGE 177:   **"Poland was not"** Weigel, *Witness to Hope*, 295.

PAGE 177–178:   **"In particular"** John Paul II, *Return to Poland*, 126.

PAGE 178:   **"fever pitch . . . and wept"** Weigel, *Witness to Hope*, 317.

PAGE 178:   **"in the spiritual history"** John Paul *II*, *Return to Poland*, 171.

PAGE 179:   **"You must be strong"** Ibid., 173.

PAGE 179:   **"And so, before I"** Ibid., 174.

PAGE 179–180:   **"So, before going"** Ibid., 174–75.

PAGE 180:   **"I hope, I hope"** Weigel, *Witness to Hope*, 321.

PAGE 180:   **"The future of Poland"** Kwitney, *Man of the Century*, 327.

PAGE 180:   **they had the dignity** Weigel, *Witness to Hope*, 321.

Permissions

Analytical Clarity: Dwight D. Eisenhower, 1944

The Stillness of Intuition: Jane Goodall, 1960

Catharsis: Ulysses S. Grant, 1864

"A Sublime Power to Rise Above": Winston Churchill, 1938

"No Never Alone": Martin Luther King Jr., 1956

Index

A Note on the Authors

Raymond M. Kethledge is a judge on the United States Court of Appeals for the Sixth Circuit, to which he was appointed in 2008, at age forty-one. He also teaches a seminar on writing and oral advocacy at the University of Michigan Law School, formerly served as a law clerk to Justice Anthony Kennedy and to Judge Ralph B. Guy Jr., and founded his own law firm with two partners. Ray received a bachelor's degree from the University of Michigan and a law degree from the University of Michigan Law School. He lives with his family near Ann Arbor, Michigan.

Michael S. Erwin received a bachelor's degree from West Point and a master's degree in psychology from the University of Michigan. He deployed to Iraq once and to Afghanistan twice. Mike is the CEO of the Character & Leadership Center, which helps to build stronger leaders through a deeper understanding of character. He is also the cofounder and president of the Positivity Project, a nonprofit organization that helps America's youth to build strong relationships in their lives by recognizing the character strengths in themselves and others. In 2010, Mike founded Team Red, White & Blue, a nonprofit dedicated to enriching veterans' lives, for which he is Chairman of the Board. Mike continues to serve as a Major in the U.S. Army Reserve, assigned to West Point's Leadership Department. He lives with his family in Pinehurst, North Carolina.